NEYRANGESTAN

A list of published works of this author by this press
appears at the end of this volume

Sadeq Hedayat
(1903 - 1951)

Sadeq Hedayat

NEYRANGESTAN

Translated from the Persian by
M. R. Ghanoonparvar

Mazda Publishers
Since 1980
2025

Publication of this book was made possible by a grant from
The A. K. Jabbari Trust

Mazda Publishers, Inc.
Academic publishers since 1980
P.O. Box 2603
Costa Mesa, California 92628 U.S.A.
www.mazdapublishers.com
A. K. Jabbari, Publisher

Library of Congress Control Number: 2024951677
ISBN 10: 1-56859-410-0
ISBN 13: 978-1-56859-410-1
Softcover (alk. paper)

This translation was supported by funds from the
Persian Heritage Foundation (PHF) Research Grant Program

CONTENTS

Translator's Foreword

Sadeq Hedayat's *Neyrangestan* is his most comprehensive work in connection with his lifelong interest in Iranian folklore. Although he records 5 April 1932 as the date of the completion of his "Introduction," *Neyrangestan* was itself published in 1933, shortly after the publication of his small book called *Owsaneh*, which is mainly a collection of popular folksongs and nursery rhymes. It seems these early efforts were due to his recent awareness of the new field of study, namely folklore, and the fact, as he mentions in his "Introduction," that although many scholars were studying the folklore of many countries, no one was doing so for Iran. At this point, however, perhaps emulating the only model he had found in Persian, a book called *Kolsum Naneh*, he merely tried to collect as many popular folksongs and nursery rhymes to publish in *Owsaneh*, and as many customs, traditions, and superstitions in *Neyrangestan*.

As Homa Katouzian aptly observes, compared to *Owsaneh*, *Neyrangestan* is "a much more substantial book, both in length and quality, though it is still short on rigour."[i] His more rigorous work in connection with folklore was published in the form of articles in *Majelleh-ye Musiqi* [*Music Magazine*], which Katouzian evaluates as follows:

> 'Folk Songs' is a studious and mature piece of research, with an introduction on the subject, both in general and in the specific case of the development of Persian folk songs. Using both Persian and European sources he discusses some of the oldest and most traditional of such Persian songs and poetical tales, and compares them with surprisingly similar folk songs and tales in European – including French, English and German – cultures. In four other pieces published in the same magazine, he reproduces four ancient children's tales, 'The Little Red-Scarf ' (Little Red

---

[i] Homa Katusian, *Sadeq Hedayat: The Life and Legend of an Iranian Writer*, 2nd edition (London: I.B. Tauris, 2022), p. 50.

Riding- Hood), 'Aqa Musheh' (Little Master Mouse), 'Shangul o Mangul' (a story of a wolf and three little goats left alone by their mother) and 'Sang-e Sabur' (The Patient Stone), two of which also exist in English.[ii]

It goes without saying that as an early attempt by Hedayat, *Neyrangestan* would hardly meet today's standards for a book on folklore studies. The value of this book, however, is that it is essentially a collection of folkloric beliefs and customs, some of which have already become obsolete, and Hedayat's penchant for collecting folkloric material has resulted in providing us with a record of them. Much of what is in this book is the result of interviews with various people, including women in various parts of the country. Hence, we should also remember that in the Iran of the late 1920s and early 1930s, it must have been quite a difficult task to gather information regarding common folk's beliefs, especially from women. Had Hedayat lived to experience the age of the Internet, his passion for folklore would have enhanced his ability to contribute greatly to Persian folklore studies. Hedayat's methodology regarding what to include in this book can be gleaned from his introduction, in which he states:

> Let me make it clear that in this book, I merely deal with beliefs and superstitions that are heard from the mouths of the common people (approximately in their own colloquial language) and I am not concerned with the supposedly valuable books in this connection, such as those on dream interpretation, the medicinal properties of animals, objects, and drugs and spices that are related to traditional medicine, or the dissertations on occult sciences. All such books are full of baseless false beliefs, and those interested in them should consult those books.

A look at the entire *Neyrangestan* makes it clear to the reader that Hedayat had been taking notes based on his first- or second-hand interviews and what he found in various books, and as he states, "it was not possible to categorize the content in a clear-cut

---

[ii] Ibid., pp. 51-52.

form." Hence, despite his attempt to categorize the notes on the basis of the table of contents he provides, there are many repetitions under various chapters. In trying to make the English text more reader friendly, without changing Hedayat's arrangement of content or the order of presentation, I have taken license as a translator to add the following to the text:

1) Within the text and in his footnotes, Hedayat sometimes provides additional information or explanations in parentheses. In all instances, my additional explanations or clarifications are added in brackets or in the Explanatory Notes at the end of the volume. The items in the Explanatory Notes are as they appear in the text.

2) In many instances, Hedayat provides subtitles for one small paragraph or even one sentence, while the following paragraph is unrelated. In some instances, when I have found it necessary for clarification, I have added a subtitle to a paragraph.

3) There are random quoted passages from various sources for some of which Hedayat provides a book title, often without full citation information. Whenever possible, I have provided the relevant information either in brackets or in the Explanatory Notes.

4) I have italicized all verses, whether quoted from well-known poets or from popular songs.

5) In a number of instances, there are either beginning or end quotation marks but no corresponding quotation marks for the same passage in the Persian text, which I have corrected whenever possible.

6) The Persian traditional weight measure "*man*" differs in certain parts of Iran. The Isfahan *man* is 6 kilograms while the Tabriz *man* is 3 kilograms. I have used the archaic English weight measure, "stone" (6.35 kg) for the Persian *man* since *man* is also becoming obsolete.

7) I have added the subtitle to the title of the book.

8) Although at the end of his introduction, Hedayat promises to "add an index at the end of the book to make it easier to find specific content," the Persian original does not have an index. I have added one to this translation.

9) In his footnotes, Hedayat quotes extensively from Zoroastrian books, some of which are either translated from Middle Persian to New Persian or "Zoroastrian Persian." In translating those

passages, I have consulted various available translations in different languages.

For the rendition of the Persian names and terms in English, I have used more of a transcription rather than transliteration method, although in many instances, they are the same. I have basically followed Naser Sharifi's system in *Cataloguing Persian Works* (Chicago: American Library Association, 1959), with the following exceptions: (1) no diacritical marks are used to distinguish between consonants that are pronounced alike in Persian and represented by different letters; (2) no diacritical marks are used to distinguish between long and short vowels in Persian, hence, the long "a" in "Hafez" that is pronounced as is the "a" in "tall" and the short "a" that is pronounced as in "hat" are transcribed the same; (3) for the most part, no apostrophe (') is used to represent the letter *eyn* and the sign *hamzeh*. With few exceptions, for the transcription of Arabic titles and names containing the Arabic definite article *al*, even when they are pronounced as *ol* or *ul*, I have used *al*. In the case of a number of Persian writers' names, I have used their preferred spelling in English.

This translation is based on Sadeq Hedayat, *Neyrangestan*, 3rd printing (Tehran: Amir Kabir Publishers, 1963.)

As always in every project, I am most indebted to my wife, Diane, for her critical editing of this nearly untranslatable text and her creative versification of all the poems and the rhyming of the popular songs.

This translation was supported by funds from the Persian Heritage Foundation (PHF) Research Grant Program, for which I am most grateful.

Neyrangestan

Take the lock of hair of a moon-faced beloved
and stop the tales between us
For auspiciousness and inauspiciousness
are influenced by Saturn and Venus
Hafez

Introduction

Apparently, ancient people and old nations have more folk beliefs and superstitions than young newly-established nations. In particular, with regard to those who have had contact with various ethnic groups as a result of the mingling of their customs, temperaments, and creeds, fresher thoughts and superstitions have emerged that have remained popular generation after generation.

In addition to many centuries of history, Iran is like a caravanserai in which all human tribes—both the civilized and the barbarian peoples of ancient times, such as the Chaldeans, Assyrians, Greeks, Jews, Turks, Arabs, and Mongols—have unloaded their cargo one after another or have been in contact with and have commingled with Iranians. Hence, researching and investigating its common people's beliefs is not only worthy of scholarly and psychological attention, but it will also clarify for us certain philosophical and historical vagaries. After investigating and comparing these superstitious beliefs with those of other nations, we will be able to understand the root causes and origins of certain customs, traditions, religions, myths and beliefs. After all, such ideas have cultivated, shaped, and contributed to the survival of all religions. It is superstitions that have channeled the mind of humanity step by step throughout various historical periods; created prejudices, self-sacrifice, and hopes and fears in human beings; and are considered the greatest and oldest consolations for humans, while still they totally dominate both barbarian and civilized people regarding most of their functions in life, because humans can disregard anything other than their superstitions and beliefs. To quote a learned scholar: "Man is a superstitious animal." Once we conduct more extensive research regarding such ideas, we shall understand the truth of this subject. Nevertheless, that is beyond the scope of our present topic.

Regarding beliefs, humans do not rely on intellect as their guide; but because of their desire and need to understand the reason for the existence of things, they resort to their hearts, their emotions, and their imagination. In regard to the appearance of superstitions and myths among primitive tribes, the famous philosopher Ernst Haeckel believes that all of these superstitions stem from a natural need that appeared in the form of the principle of cause and effect in rational laws, especially those superstitions that are created as a result of such natural incidents as thunder and lightning, earthquakes, lunar and solar eclipses, and so on, which cause fear or pose a threat. The inevitability of the existence of such natural incidents which are subject to the law of cause and effect for primitive people indicates that they had inherited these beliefs from their ancestors, the great apes, as it is also seen in other vertebrates. For instance, when a dog howls in moonlight, or hears a bell and sees the movement of the clapper in the middle of it, or sees a flag flapping in the wind, such phenomena cause fear in the dog and even create a vague craving in it to know the cause of such unknown incidents and phenomena. Part of the foundation of religions should be sought among the primitive people, especially with regard to the superstitions that are the remnants of the inherited ideas of their ape ancestors, and another part is related to the worshipping of their ancestors and the various needs of their psyches and the customs and traditions to which they have become accustomed.[1]

When we compare the superstitious beliefs and thinking of barbarian, semi-civilized, and civilized nations, we gather that they have all, more or less, stemmed from the same source and have appeared in different forms. The great scholar Edward Tylor, who has done extensive research in comparing the customs, traditions, and superstitious beliefs of various nations, states:

> When we compare (the customs and beliefs of) barbarian tent-dwellers with those of civilized countries,

---

[1] [Ernst] Haeckel, *Les énigmes de l'univers*, p. 300-301.

we become astonished as to how much of certain
parts of the low civilizations can be seen and identi-
fied, with minor changes, in high civilizations, and
how they sometimes totally resemble one another.[2]

However, what is important to know is whether or not all
such strange, odd, contradictory, sometimes ridiculous, and at
other times astonishing ideas known as superstitious beliefs are
the products of indigenous thinking, and what the nature is of
their relationship to one another.

Obviously, masses of people everywhere in the world only
think about their own lives and never invent anything. But in
every era, even in very primitive environments among the pas-
sive masses who make up the majority, some individuals can be
found who think and invent. In other words, they take the ideas
and emotions of the masses and turn them into didactic state-
ments, and it is from the same class of people that the common
people obtain their knowledge and beliefs. However, it should be
noted that part of these customs and superstitions that appear to
be heinous and distasteful today have undoubtedly not been created by Iranian thinking; rather, they have been imposed on Iranians as a result of associating with alien ethnicities and are due
to the imposition of religious and external pressures. Here I will
explain this notion briefly.

Without trying to engage in a thorough investigation and
analysis of this issue in terms of their origins and sources, we
can organize these ideas into several categories. Leaving aside
secondary categorizations, which are beyond the scope this brief
introduction, I will divide them into two major categories. In the
proper context, discussing each category separately is an important matter.

1. Indigenous ideas and beliefs that are the outcome of day-
to-day familial, religious, or individual experiences or are among
the very old mementos of Indo-Iranian heritage that have sur-
vived in Iran.

Such customs and ideas can be considered Iranian, and they
are worthy of attention for research, since some of them are infi-

---

[2] E. Tylor, *Civilisation primitive*, vol. 1, p. 8. [Edward B. Tylor, *Primitive Culture*].

nitely old and might be left behind from primitive periods of
human life and the time of the migration of the Aryan tribes to
the Iranian plateau, such as beliefs and myths regarding the
moon, the sun, dragons, speaking with animals and plants, and so
on, the origin and the source of which are undoubtedly quite old.
For instance, speaking with trees[3] shows that at the time, not only did people believe that plants have a soul and are alive, but
they also believed that the plants were intelligent and assumed
that they understood human speech. In the philosophy of the Zoroastrian religion, there is a hierarchy of souls, and all beings
have a *farvahar*, or spirit; but Zoroastrianism does not believe
that plants have intelligence. This shows that this belief existed
prior to the advent of Zoroastrianism. The same is true regarding
speaking with animals[4] and belief in stones, trees,[5] objects, and
other things as manifestations of the incarnation of the soul.

Another matter is revealing good fortune or bad fortune as
practiced by common people regarding the singing of birds, certain incidents and accidents, the shape of objects, as well as good
luck and bad luck, good omen and bad omen, and so on, all of
which belong to this category, and they have become popular
incidentally and when they have been verified by the experiences
of one or a few individuals. All nations in the world have such
fortunetelling beliefs which are very similar.

On the other hand, we see that Zoroastrianism initially op-
poses superstitions, and the Avesta becomes distrustful and at-
tacks the sorcerers and superstitions that have become widespread in Iran due to the influence of Turanians. The Avesta calls
the sorcerers demons and issues instructions for preventing their

---

[3] See the chapter, "Plants and Seeds."
[4] In colloquial Persian, animals are addressed as *"zaban basteh"*
[tongue-tied]. This shows that common people consider animals to
have intelligence and assume that their silence is due to the inability to
speak. Stories about the metamorphosis of animals verify this. Indigenous people of America and Africa believe that the great apes converse
with one another, but when they are in the presence of humans, they
pretend to be ignorant and keep silent, so that they would not be forced
to work.
[5] "Wish trees" exist in most Iranian cities and villages. See the chapter,
"Famous Places and Things."

heinous acts,[6] including the hiding of teeth, fingernails and toe-nails, and head hair to prevent access to sorcerers. It is unclear whether or not at the time when this part of the Avesta was written,[7] sorcerers had a great deal of influence, and this ruling was issued against them.[8]

Several books survive from the Sassanid era which clearly reveal the existence of such beliefs at that time. They include *Arda-Virazh-Nameh*, *Shayast Neshayast*, *Denkard*, *Bundahishn*, and the book of *Neyrangestan*, which is similar to ordinary prayer books and claims astonishing effects for certain prayers.[9] Another book is *Sad Dar Bundehesh*, which has been published in Persian in India and is from a relatively more recent date than the above-mentioned books. This book has many notes, most of which are the same folkloric beliefs, some of which are still widespread, such as respect for the lamp, respect for bread, the effect of the evil eye,[10] Persian New Year rituals, the *Haft Sin* [Seven S's] table, and so on, which will be discussed later in this book.

2. Beliefs and superstitions of foreign people—such as the Sakas, Parthians, Greeks, Romans, and in particular Semitic people such as the Chaldeans, Babylonians, Jews, and Arabs—which have come to Iran and consequently have been imposed on the people by religion, or are the distortions of indigenous customs that have been altered to appear alien.

Without intending to engage in a historical discussion, these effects began from the time of the Achaemenids and the influential role of the Magi in Zoroastrian religion, because we know that most of them were from foreign ethnic groups, such as the

---

[6] See the Avesta, chapter 17, as well as the footnote to [the chapter in this book on] "Fortunetelling by Body Parts."

[7] The oldest part of the Avesta, scholars believe, consists of the Gathas, to which other parts were added later.

[8] There were even the effects of Egyptian superstitions in ancient Iran. Among the objects discovered during numerous excavations in Susa, the National Museum of Iran houses an Egyptian evil eye talisman, a sacred eye made of baked porcelain with a blue glazed surface.

[9] Since the subject matter of the present volume is similar to that of the Sassanid era book, I have used it for the title of this work.

[10] In the Avesta, the demon of the evil eye is called "Aghashi," and in the *Bundahishn*, the same demon is called "Ghash."

Sakas, the Parthians, and the Semites, who engaged in astrology, fortunetelling, and sorcery. Eventually, they were the ones who weakened Zoroastrianism, because of the superstitious beliefs they attached to it. As an example, I will cite the following from the book of Chaldean fortunetelling authored by F. Lenormant:

> The wooden sticks which the Chaldeans, and imitating them the Arabs, used for fortunetelling resembled tamarisk tree branches which the Median Magi used for the same purpose... When the Magi became influential in the Zoroastrian religion, they made the use of a *barsam* [tree branch used in Zoroastrian religious prayers and rituals] customary. Despite the fact that the spirit of the religion of Zoroaster abhors and shuns fortunetelling and superstitions, a *barsam* is a necessary part of the rituals of the Zoroastrian priests who have remained faithful to the religion of their ancestors.[11]

In a footnote, he adds that in the ancient parts of the Avesta, no mention is made of a *barsam*[12] and its uses.

In contrast, neighbors such as Chaldea and Assyria, which can be called the mothers of superstitions and sorcery—with their terrifying gods, sacrifices, good and bad omen days and hours, the effect of the stars on the destiny of mankind—all together had an effect on Iran, although Iranians were less susceptible than their neighbors to believing in superstitions. In addition to those, the invasion by the Greeks, with their oracles,

---

[11] F. Lenormant, *Divination*, pp., 22-23. [*La divination et la science des présages chez la Chaldéens*, by François Lenormant; translation: *The Magic And Sorcery Of The Chaldeans*, by Francois Lenormant.]

[12] "*Barsam* consists of thin, one-handspan-long branches which are cut from manna and ephedra trees, and if those trees are not available, from a pomegranate tree, and the custom for cutting it is that first they thoroughly wash a *barsam* cutter, which is a knife with an iron handle, then they whisper [a prayer]... Whenever they want to read a chapter of the Avesta or to worship or to wash their bodies or to eat food, they hold a few *barsam*s in their hand, and when they eat, they hold five *barsam*s in their hand, and one of the requirements for holding *barsam*s in their hand is to have clean bodies and wear clean clothes." From *Jahangiri Dictionary*.

gods, and demi-gods, and then being neighbors to the Romans, with their astrologers, interpreters of dreams, and stargazers, in addition to the migration of the Jews and the superstitious beliefs that they brought as souvenirs from Egypt and the deserts of Arabia, and finally the invasion of the Arabs, all solidified the foundation for such superstitions in Iran.

Because of their kinship with the Arabs, the Jews took advantage of the situation and greatly contributed to the spreading of superstitions. Hadith scribes, chroniclers, and a bunch of superstition fabricators joined them and propagated decadent superstitious ideas through the mouths of common people.[13] Numerous books containing ideas of this sort are extant, and most of them have unfortunately been published and have filled the bookstores of the farmers' markets.

The thinking and the lives of people in general, and women in particular, changed after the advent of Islam, because they were enslaved by men and became housebound; polygamy became widespread; and the injection of fatalistic ideas, religious mourning, and sadness and sorrow turned the minds of the people toward sorcery, talismans, prayers, and jinn, diminishing their ability for work and effort. All this led the way to the production of a new series of superstitious beliefs.

Blood-spilling religious pledges and animal sacrifices and all the protocols related to them resulted in such barbarian customs stemming from the worship of masters and others, which undoubtedly are the outcome of Semitic minds. Since the ignorant primitive man was frightened by the forces of nature and considered himself a victim of the wrath of nature, he imagined any one of these forces to be a bloodthirsty god; and in order to lessen that god's wrath, he imagined this exchange and trade would spare his own life. In other words: don't kill me, instead eat this animal. This was the stroke of genius of the Semitic mind that belonged to the Chaldeans, the Jews, and the Arabs. There is no precedent for bloody sacrifices in Aryan religions.[14]

---

[13] One of the important chroniclers of Islamic events was a Jewish man by the name of Ka'b al-Ahbar (*History of Tabari*).

[14] On the whole, tormenting and torturing animals was not an Iranian custom and was imported from outside. Even harmful creatures, such as locusts, snakes, and ants, the killing of which, according to histori-

That which is worthy of note is that not only did alien people bring an abundance of superstitious beliefs to Iran, but also
they made great efforts to eliminate all that was Iranian or
change everything that was of Iranian origin into alien ideas. For
instance, the Greek Alexander, who has gained an unwarranted
reputation in Persian literature, is the same person who referred
to Iranians as "cursed," and after the advent of Islam, he acquired a specious prophet-like status. If we compare Alexander
with Rostam, we shall see that most of the forged legends that
they attribute to Alexander resemble those stories of the famed
Rostam. For Rostam, the head of the White Demon was his hel-
met, and the Arabs translate Alexander as *Dhu al-Qaarnayn* [He
of the Two Horns].[15] The legend of the Water of Life and the
travel of Alexander to the Realm of Darkness is not dissimilar to
the Seven Feats of Rostam, which is an Iranian legend.[16]

Qows-e qazah [rainbow], also known as Ali's bow, was
known as Rostam's bow in ancient times.[17] There are many
changes made of this sort by which Iranian myths and history are
distorted and disguised and have assumed a foreign hue. For instance, the tomb of Cyrus the Great in Morghab has been desig-
nated as the tomb of the mother of Solomon; the attribution of
Divband [Demon Conqueror] to Solomon, despite the fact that
all evidence shows that Tahmures was known as *Divband*, thus,
the attribution of such power to Solomon, who was Jewish, is
absolutely false and forged. The handwritten manuscript of *Salaman and Absal* states:

---

ans, was considered commendable, was the invention of the Magi, who
were often of an alien race. The best evidence is that Ferdowsi, who
was quite familiar with the philosophy, spirit, and customs of ancient
Iran, states:

> *Do not harm the ant that carries a seed*
> *A live ant, enjoying its own sweet life, indeed*
> *He who intends to cause an ant in sorrow to moan*
> *Has a mind that is dark and a heart made of stone*
> *Would it please you and would you agree*
> *To take life away whilst alive you would be?*

[15] This point was mentioned by Z. Behruz.
[16] See the chapter on "Common Folk Myths," in particular, the pages
where Jabalqa and Jabalsa and Gang Dezh are discussed.
[17] See the chapter on "Common Folk Myths."

Solomon ben David was an Israeli prophet after Moses and before Jesus. There is no mention of *div* [de-
mon] or *angoshtar* [ring] neither in the Torah nor the
Bible. Soleyman is a Persian word for Solomon. That
is why Jamshid was thought to be Solomon and on
that basis, whatever historians have attributed to Solomon has been from Jamshid. Solomon was an author and wrote several books on religious laws, which
are available to Jews, Christians, and Muslims. Such
attributions are found neither in his own books nor in
the books of history of Jews and Christians, because
the name of the son of Jam was Solomon.[18]

The History of Tabarestan [by Isfandiyar, 1905] states: "It
is reported in the news of the companions that when the Prophet
Solomon caught the owner of the ring, he imprisoned him in the
Jinn-Haunted Rock (on Mount Damavand)." The author of
Ajayeb al-Makhluqat [Wonders of Creation] repeats the same
story, whereas according to all extant documents and narratives
from ancient times, Fereydun imprisoned Zahhak on Mount
Damavand. It is not clear by whose provocation and invention
Solomon has inherited and become the substitute for all the
names in Iranian mythology. Relentless efforts have been made
to erase the ancient mementos from the memories of the people.[19]

---

[18] It is stated in the *Denkard* that Kaykavus ruled seven countries, and
all humans, demons, and fairies obeyed him, and by a mere gesture
from him, they carried out his orders. In *Yana Bei' al-Islam* [Sources of
Islam], p. 215, it is stated: "... and in addition to all this, it is clear that
in this Zoroastrian volume (Yasht 19, Verses 30-31), it is written regarding Jamshid that he ruled over humans, jinn, fiends and others. Of
course, what the Jews say regarding the Prophet Solomon in the same
vein has been from the same source, and Muslims have acquired the
same story from them."
[19] Mas'udi says in *Moravej [al-Zahab wa Ma'aden al-Jowhar]* [Mead-
ows of Gold and Mines of Gems] (Volume 2, p. 118) that the details of
all the events of the history of Iran and its myths, such as those regarding Rostam, Siyavash and others, are recorded in detail in a book entitled *Al-Seksiran* (Seksiran, or Leaders of Sistan), which was translated
from the ancient language of Iran into Arabic by Ibn Muqaffa'. Appar-

Of the same kind are also myths that have gone from Iran to other places and after some changes have turned into a new form, more or less, such as *'Alf Laylah wa-Laylah* [*One Thousand and One Nights*], which is a rendition of *Hezar Afsan* of the Sassanid era and which was translated from Pahlavi into Arabic, and the Arabs made many changes to it.

In addition to what has already been mentioned, there are many superstitions that were fabricated and falsely authenticated as a result of the inventions or impositions of mythmakers, hadith writers and chroniclers, soothsaying astrologers, sorcerers, and prayer-charm writers, who enjoyed popularity among the common people, and some of these superstitions were devised by sly individuals for personal gain, amusement, or out of ignorance. For example, one of the European superstitious beliefs that reportedly was fabricated during the World War and has now had an impact on the Europeanized class in Tehran is that you should not light three cigarettes with one match, because the person with the third cigarette will die. The popular story is that on the battlefield, the third soldier who lit his cigarette with the same match would be the target of an enemy bullet. Another version of the story is that Kreuger, the merchant of matches, promoted this idea among the people to sell more merchandise. After a while, however, the original source of that belief or myth was forgotten and the belief alone remains. The myth of "hunger disease"[20] and the story of the elephant who became the king of India[21] are good examples regarding the creation of superstitions. What is noteworthy, however, is that among these common people's ideas, we come across sayings and rules that the common people have devised against superstitious thinking, such as: "Shave your head and clip your nails every day, since nothing is better than that"; "Someone lost money on Wednesday eve, someone else found money on Wednesday"; and, "All months come with danger, but people only blame it on the month of Safar."

---

ently, Islamic historians and report scribes made abundant use of this book.

[20] See the chapter on "Conventions Regarding Ailments."

[21] See the final pages of the chapter on "Domestic and Wild Animals."

Let me make it clear that in this book, I merely deal with beliefs and superstitions that are heard from the mouths of the common people (approximately in their own colloquial language) and I am not concerned with the supposedly valuable books in this connection, such as those on dream interpretation, the medicinal properties of animals, objects, and drugs and spices that are related to traditional medicine,[22] or the dissertations on occult sciences. All such books are full of baseless false beliefs, and those interested in them should consult those books.

The only book regarding common people's customs and traditions is the famous book, *Kolsum Naneh* [akin to Old Wives Tales], written by Mr. Jamal Khonsari, which has been translated into foreign languages and its original Persian edition is available everywhere. Nevertheless, some of the material in that book seems exaggerated, since we should not forget that most of such customs and superstitious beliefs are obsolete and have been eliminated nowadays; and interestingly, even old women regard them as ridiculous.

Like all sorts of beliefs and ideas, superstitions also have their own life. Sometimes they appear and replace other superstitions, and at another time, they disappear. Progress in sciences, new ideas, and time help greatly in this connection. It often happens that one group of superstitions is eliminated by them, while another group is much harder to replace. Of course, if left alone, they retain their supernatural aspect for a long time, because the common people consider them as Divine revelations and transmit them to one another. For eliminating such superstitious beliefs, nothing is better than publishing them in order to undermine their importance and credibility and reveal their baselessness. In particular, each needs to be investigated separately, because we should not be under the false impression that such dec-

---

[22] In *Ajayeb al-Makhluqat*, it is stated: "If someone eats the flesh of parrots, he becomes eloquent." From this type of strange and odd properties ascribed in old books to things that exist, we can assess that since the parrot imitates human speech, they had thought that eating its flesh makes people eloquent. This idea resembles that of the Australian aboriginal peoples who think that if someone eats the heart of a tiger, he becomes braver. Eating the heart of a tiger and bravery is a more fitting analogy than the flesh of a parrot and eloquence. Besides, this idea was fabricated and is not considered a part of common people's thinking.

adent thinking will be eliminated on its own. It often happens that those who otherwise shun all dogmatic beliefs become unraveled when it comes to the issue of superstitions. This is due to the fact that common women have whispered these ideas into the ears of children, who grow up and then they can assess whether or not to accept or reject any idea, with the exception of superstitious beliefs, because they have been inculcated into their brains in childhood and they have never been able to examine them rationally. For this reason, such beliefs always retain their impact and continuously become stronger, and such people react to any objection by saying "augury is augury, whether good or bad."

In his comprehensive book, Tylor concludes:

> The wisdom of the classes of the people has another responsibility which is very important and difficult, and that is, it must remove the concealing cover from that which is left in our society in the form of unfortunate superstitious beliefs from inferior violent civilizations in ancient times, and eliminate and uproot them all at once. Even though this task is not very pleasant, it is necessary and compulsory for the peace and tranquility of human society. In this way, the study of civilizations, in the same way that it has seriously strived for and assisted the progress of the society, must also take steps to sever and break asunder the chains that have enslaved it. This science is especially for leaders who stand up to strive for modernizing and reforming the society.[23]

Moreover, there is no doubt that until such ideas are codified separately as superstitious beliefs, foreigners will consider these baseless beliefs as part of our national customs, whereas codifying them as archaic beliefs conveys their obsolescence and lack of importance.

Nevertheless, we should not forget that some of these customs and traditions are not only fine and acceptable, but they are mementos of Iran's glorious past. Among them are the Festival of Mehregan, the Festival of Nowruz, the Festival of Sadeh, Chaharshanbeh Suri, and so on, the revival and maintaining of

---

[23] E. Tylor, *Civilization Primitive* [*Primitive Culture*] II, p. 681.

which is considered an important national duty, and we must consider a separate status for them. For example, making bonfires, similar to "carnivals," has existed from ancient times, just as it is a custom and is of interest to Europeans. Wedding ceremonies and celebrations, jubilees, cleanliness, harmless humorous ideas, and enjoyable literary legends on the whole have a positive effect on our lives and show the long life of a nation that has gotten too old, has contemplated a great deal, and has had numerous poetic ideas. On the other hand, the superstitious beliefs that have been imported to Iran from abroad make life difficult and toxic, such as believing in good omen and bad omen hours, animal sacrifices, good omens and bad omens of stars, belief in fate, and so on.

Today, in all civilized countries, groups of scholars have collected the superstitious beliefs of all nations, including the civilized countries and the primitive tribes of Africa and Australia, in hundreds of books. By comparing them, a new field of knowledge has been created called "folklore," which is of great interest to scholars in many fields, especially in psychology and psychoanalysis, the history of civilizations, the history of religions, and so on. Interestingly, however, it is surprising that thus far, Iran's common people's customs, traditions and beliefs have not been collected, with the exception of a brief account of them in *Kolsum Naneh*. What one can find in published books consists of some superstitious beliefs, whether true or not, which European travelers have recorded in their books.

For now, as a first step, I will offer this collection, which comprises a brief account of the knowledge of Iran's common people, as a complement to a small book that was published in the same series as that entitled *Owsaneh*. I hope to complete this study in the future and also to publish a collection of folk tales. I would like to express my profound gratitude to Dr. Partow, Mr. Javad Kamalian, Mr. A. Moqaddam, Mirza Hoseyn Khan Mo'ini-Kermani, Mr. H. Yaghma'i, Mr. P. Alavi, Mr. Z. Hashtrudi, Mr. "P" from Khorasan, and many others who have generously provided me with their assistance. I am especially indebted to Mr. Mojtaba Minovi, who, in addition to all his help, shared his valuable notes with me.

Given that it was not possible to categorize the content in a clear-cut form, since many of the beliefs would be repeated several times, in order to avoid repetition, I will add an index at the end of the book to make it easier to find specific content.

Tehran-5 April 1932
S. Hedayat

1

Marriage Customs and Ceremonies

Marriage Contract Protocols

The room in which marriage contract protocols are performed must be built on solid ground. All the women who are present in the room must be happily married. A white supper cloth is spread in the direction of the Qibla. The mirror sent by the bridegroom (good fortune mirror) is placed at the top of the supper cloth, with two candelabras, one placed on each side, in which they light one candle in the name of the bride and another candle in the name of the groom. A handful of wheat is sprinkled in front of the mirror, and then it is covered with a cashmere cloth. Then they light an oil lamp filled with honey and oil. A flat washtub is placed upside down on it, and a horse saddle is placed on top of the washtub for the bride to sit on.

During the recital of the marriage contract vows, the bride looks into the mirror. Her clothes must not have any knots. The strings of her clothes must not be knotted, so that she would never have a knot in her affairs.

The following items are necessary for the marriage contract supper cloth:

A copy of the Koran, a prayer rug, a glazed earthen punch bowl of sherbet, a large loaf of *sangak* bread, a large wooden tray the surface of which is decorated with designs made with wild rue, flatbread with goat cheese and fresh herbs, walnuts, mercury, a bowl of water with a green leaf floating on the surface, two sugar cones which are rubbed together over the head of the bride when the Sermon of Adam[1] is recited, fruits and sweets. Seven gems are ground in a mortar; vinegar is boiled

---

[1] Prayers recited during the performance of marriage contract vows.

mixed with lye along with white pepper in a coffee urn, and in another coffee urn two eggs are boiled with seven spices, wishing for children. One of the eggs is eaten by the bride and the other by the groom. A person using a string of seven colors symbolically ties the tongue of the bride's mother-in-law and sister-in-law, and they pound the floor next to the feet of the bride with a symbolic tongue made of thin red cloth and say, "I tied the tongues of mother-in-law, sister-in-law, the wife of the groom's brother, and father-in-law."

At the same time, someone constantly locks and unlocks a lock, and as soon as the recitation of the prayer is completed, she locks it, and in order to prevent the groom from becoming acquainted with another woman, it must not be unlocked before the wedding night celebrations and the consummation of the marriage.

The core of a hazelnut is taken out, the shell is filled with mercury, the hole is covered with beeswax, and it is sent along with the bride, so that in the same way that mercury slides back and forth in the hazelnut shell, the heart of the groom will also palpitate for the bride.

After the completion of the marriage contract ceremony, the water in the bowl is poured over the head of the bride and the candles are extinguished with her shoes.

The seven gems and mercury are for good fortune; water represents light; the green leaf means a pleasant life; for the bride, sitting on a saddle is for making her dominate her husband; honey and oil make everything smooth and sweet; wild rue is for good omen; bread and goat cheese and fresh herbs bring blessing, and if the people present eat them, they will never suffer from toothache.

Wedding Night Celebration

The bride's dowry is delivered to the groom's house. First, the mirror, the Koran, and a tulip-shaped candelabra are taken into the house, and they sprinkle wild rue on a brazier of charcoal fire to burn and smoke, as a sign of good omen.

On the night of the wedding celebration, specific wedding songs are sung.[2]

---

[2] See *Owsaneh*, first printing, pp. 24-25.

When they are taking the bride to the groom's house, a pre-pubescent boy ties bread and goat cheese to her waist, and they also place an old shoe of the bride next to her in the carriage for good luck. When they bring the bride, the groom must step forward to welcome her. During the welcoming process, the groom tosses a bitter orange toward the bride. If the bride is able to catch it, she will be dominant over the groom. When the bride enters the husband's house, she says "Oh sweetheart of God" in order to become his sweetheart. The groom must go on the top of the courtyard gate of the house for the bride to walk underneath him, in order for him to dominate her. When the groom enters the bridal chamber, they place the bride's shoes above the door for the groom to pass under. On that night, all the women who have gathered in that house are religiously allowed to be seen by the groom without their veils, and anyone who picks up the sweet nuggets that they toss over the bride and groom while cheering will have his or her problems solved. When they place the hand of the bride in the hand of the groom, the one who is able to step on the foot of the other will have a longer tongue to dominate the other. After they have placed the hand of the bride in the groom's hand, they tie the big toes of the bride and groom together and wash them with rosewater. This action, however, requires great skill. If the big toe of one gets on top of the big toe of the other, he or she will become dominant over the other. Then, the groom tosses gold coins into the flat washtub, gives a gift to the bride for unveiling her face for the first time, and splashes the rosewater on the wall, to bring blessing to the house.

The bride and groom's bedding must be spread by a woman who has been married only once, whose husband is alive, and who has no co-wives. On the morning after the consummation of the marriage, the family of the bride sends her *kachi-ye ghigh-nagh*, which is made with eggs cooked with brown sugar.

On the night when the marriage is being consummated, a woman from the family of the bride must sleep in front of the bridal chamber.

On the morning after the consummation of the marriage, when they take the groom to the public bathhouse, a groom's mate, that is, a prominent male member of the groom's family who has not married yet, must accompany him shoulder to shoulder everywhere. That man will soon be married. The bride also must have a bridesmaid. Becoming a bridesmaid brings about luck in finding a good husband.

2

Pregnant Women

Chellehbori

To get pregnant, water is taken from the four corners of the public bathhouse in eggshells and poured it on the head of the woman who wants to get pregnant.

Things that Affect the Unborn

If a pregnant woman scratches any part of her body during a solar or lunar eclipse, that part of the baby will get a permanent birthmark.

If a pregnant woman bites into an apple, her baby's lip will get a dimple.

If anyone is cooking an aromatic food, they must give some of it to any pregnant woman who might smell it. If they do not, the baby's eyes will become blue, and they will be morally indebted to that baby.

Whenever a pregnant woman is looking at someone and the baby moves in her womb (in the direction of that person), the baby will look like that person.

In Azerbaijan, people believe that if a pregnant woman takes food from someone, her baby will look like that person; for this reason, pregnant women should avoid taking food from people they do not know.

A nine-month pregnant woman who passes under a camel that is part of a caravan will give birth at ten months.

When a pregnant woman wakes up in the morning, the broom behind the door starts trembling and says to itself, "I am sure she is going to eat me today."[1]

---

[1] Pregnant women need to eat a lot.

Boy or Girl

A pregnant woman whose face develops vitiligo will give birth to a girl.

If a pregnant woman finds a safety pin in an alleyway, her baby will be a girl, and if she finds a needle, it will be a boy.

If saltwater is poured on a pregnant woman's head without her realizing it, and then if she touches her lips, her baby will be a boy, and if she touches her hair, her baby will be a girl.

If the expressed milk of a pregnant woman is poured in water and it goes to the bottom, her baby will be a boy, and if it stays on the surface, it will be a girl.[2]

If a pregnant woman eats a lot of apples, her baby will be a boy; if her cravings are for pickles, the baby will be a girl; and if she is more inclined toward sweets, the baby will be a boy.

Any woman who eats the food remaining on the supper cloth will give birth to a boy.

A pair of scissors and a knife are placed in front of a pregnant woman and she closes her eyes; if she picks up the scissors, her baby will be a girl, and if she picks up the knife, her baby will be a boy.

A pregnant woman who works a lot and walks a lot will have a boy, and if she just eats and sleeps, her baby will be a girl.

Triplets

If a woman gives birth to three daughters in one pregnancy, it will be pleasing to the king at the time.

Predicting the Number of Children

The number of bumps around a woman's nipples will reveal the number of children she will have.

---

[2] "If they want to know whether a pregnant woman is carrying a girl or a boy, they should express the milk of the pregnant woman on the palm of the hand and drop a louse in it. If the louse gets out, it will be a girl, otherwise it will be a boy, because the milk of a girl is thin and the louse can get through it, and the milk of a boy is thick, and it cannot pass through it. This is an analogy the truth of which only God Almighty knows." From *Nozhat al-Qolub*.

Sharing Eggs
If eggs are eaten in front of a woman who is with child, she must be given some. Otherwise, the person eating them will be morally indebted to her.

Traditional Prediction of Baby's Gender
"If you want to know whether a pregnant woman is carrying a boy or a girl, beckon her. If she steps forward with her right foot, she will have a boy, and if with the left foot, she will have a girl. Another method: If the right breast of the woman grows larger, it will be a boy, and if her left breast gets larger first, it will be a girl. If her nipples are red, the baby will be a boy, and if they are dark, it will be a girl. Another method: If the pregnant woman is nimble, smiling, and good tempered, the baby will be a boy; and if she is grumpy, has a sour face, is lazy and bad tempered, the baby will be a girl. God is the knowledgeable one."[3]

How to Make Perfect Babies
"And it is said that when the notables wanted intimacy with a woman or a female slave, they would wear a golden belt and command the woman to wear adornments and jewelry. They said that if such is done, the offspring will be brave with a beautiful face, wise, and pleasant in the hearts of the people; and when you give birth to a son, his cradle should be adorned with gold and silver, which they would say are both the lords of the people."[4]

Locking the Abdomen
A string is tied around the waist of a pregnant woman who is spotting [too early] or is at risk, and a lock is put at the ends. Then, the "Yasin" chapter of the Koran is recited, and at each of the seven repetitions of the word *mobeyn* [clearly], they blow on the lock and lock it. Then they unlock the lock at nine months.

Pain and Labor
If the pregnant woman is in great pain, wrapping a blessing (supper cloth) on her belly will ameliorate her pain. A midwife

[3] *Hezar Asrar ya Rahnema-ye Eshrat*, p. 6.
[4] *Nowruznameh*, p. 25.

addresses the unborn baby: "Come out! Hurry up. We have prepared warm water for washing you. We have sewn new clothes
for you. What are you waiting for?" They pawn the black chador
of the pregnant woman, use the money to buy dates, and give
them away as alms. They drop cyclamen in water; they perform
the call to prayers; the husband pours water in the lap of his
clothes and makes her drink it; and after delivery, they rub ce-
ruse on her and put a beauty mark between her eyebrows.

Prohibition
A woman who has lost a child must not enter a pregnant
woman's room.

Al
Al [pronounced as "all"] is an imaginary creature in the
shape of a woman with scrawny, bony arms and legs and a red
face, whose nose is made of clay. Here is a verse about her from
some poet:

> *Her color is red and her nose of clay*
> *If you confront such a creature, keep her at bay*
> *Grab her and quickly tie her to prevent from the start*
> *Her stealing a pregnant woman's liver and heart*

What Al does is that she takes the liver of a woman who has
recently delivered a baby, places it in a basket, and takes it away.
As long as the woman's liver has not passed over water, she will
recover. To ward off the danger of Al, people put five or three
onions on a skewer and place it in the corner of the room. It is
also good to have a rifle and a sword in a pregnant woman's
room.[5] They place a black woolen rope around the pregnant
woman's bed, and they stick on the walls around the room
twelve cotton wicks, one side of which is white and the other
side smeared black by rubbing them on the outside of cooking
pots. This frightens Al.

According to another account, the birthing mother's bed
must not be red. Barley should be poured on the birthing moth-

---

[5] On the whole, the jinn are afraid of iron and reciting the name of God.
For this reason, ironware is an effective way to drive away the jinn.

er's lap and a horse should eat it. With an unsheathed sword, a line must be drawn around her bed and the following words uttered: "For whom am I drawing a fence? For Maryam and her baby. Draw it. Congratulations."[6] Then they place the unsheathed sword above the birthing mother's head until the day she goes to the public bathhouse after giving birth.

On the tenth day after delivery, when she goes to the bathhouse, they take the skewered onions with her, and on the steps of the public bathhouse, they take out the onions and have them smashed under her foot, or they break a walnut under her foot and toss the onions in flowing water. [In the bathhouse], they pour water over her head with a "forty-key" bowl. After the bath, Al cannot harm the mother who has recently delivered when she is alone.

---

[6] In *Kolsum Naneh*, the quoted statement is as follows: "I draw it with a scratching sound, I draw it with a scratching sound, I draw it with many scratching sounds and scratching sounds."

3

Children

On Babies

When a baby is born, it is washed, and then they take a piece of calico and cut it in order to put it over the baby's head and cover the baby with it. They call this clothing a Resurrection Day shirt. The baby must wear it for one night and one day. Then, they wrap the baby in white swaddling clothes and put it to sleep in a cradle. They hang the cradle over a clay bread oven and pour some uncooked rice in the cradle, which later they give to a beggar. On the seventh day after the birth of the baby, when the midwife cuts the umbilical cord, she receives a tip.

A candle is lit above the head of a newborn for ten days, and on the tenth day, they pour tenth-day water over its head from a "forty-key" bowl.[1]

---

[1] "(1) When a woman in a household becomes pregnant, it is necessary to endeavor to maintain a continual fire in that house, and to continue to watch over it. (2) And, once the infant becomes separated from the mother, it is necessary to burn a lamp for three nights and days—to burn a fire would be better—to prevent the demons and fiends from being able to do any damage or harm; because, when a child is born, it is exceedingly fragile for those three days. (3) For it is declared in revelation that when Zoroaster of the Spitaman clan was separated from his mother, every night for three nights, a demon came, along with 150 other demons, so that they might cause the slaughter of Zoroaster, and when they beheld the light of the fire, they fled away, unable to do any damage or harm. (4) During the first forty days, it is not proper to leave the infant alone; and it is also not proper for the mother of the infant to step over a threshold in the dwelling, or to cast her eyes upon a mountain, for such is bad for her." *Sad Dar* 16, p. 15.

When a child is born, they must put it to sleep on the ground for six nights, and on the seventh night, the birthing mother herself should put the baby in the cradle. That night is called the "Auspicious Night," and they must have sweets and foods ready. The midwife must tie the baby's hand behind it with a handkerchief and feed the baby a little of the abovementioned eatables and tell those present, "Take the baby!" (Someone should take it and hand it to another.) The last one should say, "May God protect the baby."[2]

When they name the baby on the sixth night, the baby should not be put on the ground. On that night, they must cook *sheshandaz*. If the baby is given the name of one of the twelve imams, that imam will intercede on his or her behalf on Resurrection Day.[3]

If the vertebra of a very fat child are counted, the child will die.

A person carrying written prayers should not enter a baby's room unless he or she leaves the written prayers outside.

If the baby jacket of the first child survives, they put it on other children for good luck.

If a baby is born on a Friday, they must weigh it and give away as charity the same weight in dates. Otherwise, the eldest in the family will die.

If someone has seven daughters, it is an ill omen to have a son.

If a nursing mother becomes stressed and bad tempered, her milk becomes contaminated and is harmful for the baby.

A child who is born on the day of the Feast of Sacrifices receives the title of Hajji [aka: Haji].

A baby that cries a lot will have a good singing voice.

If a baby sticks its tongue out a lot, the reason is that during her pregnancy, its mother had seen a snake.

---

[2] *Kolsum Naneh*, p. 14. Published in Bombay.
[3] During the Sassanid era, one of the cardinal sins was to give babies foreign, in other words non-Persian, names. The *Denkard*, 8, 15, 31. After the Islamic invasion, people used Persian and Arabic names, such as Firuz, Bahman, Hasan, Omar, and so on, indiscriminately. It appears that the ruling regarding the names of the imams was created during the Safavid era.

Parents whose children die soon or before they can walk name their last daughter Bemani Khanom [Ms. Survivor] and their last son, Aqa Mandi [Mr. Survived] or Khoda Bogzar [God let Him Be] or Mandeh Ali [Remainder of Ali].[4]

In Azerbaijan, when they have too many daughters in a family, they call the seventh one "Qezbas," which means "enough daughters," in order to have a son after her.

Babies must be concealed from people who have the evil eye.

If they lay the baby on its stomach and lift its legs from behind, either its mother or father will die.

If when a child is born, one of its relatives dies, the baby is considered an ill omen.

If a baby begins to scoot on its bottom before it can walk, the next child will be a girl.

If a baby starts to crawl on its stomach, the next child will be a boy.

If a baby tries to suck its big toe, it indicates that it wants to have a brother or sister.

The foreskin of a boy after circumcision should be roasted separately and fed to the boy so that his body is not lessened.[5]

On What Children Do

If a child touches its hair with greasy hands, it will become bald.

A child who sticks its finger in its nose will become bald.

If a small child makes itself the shape of a gate (by spreading its feet out wide with its head on the ground), it means that a guest is coming to visit.

If a small child begins to sweep the house, it means that a guest is coming to visit.

If a small child sees someone eating some fruit or food and wants some, he must be given some; otherwise, that person would be morally indebted to the child.

---

[4] It is the name for a goat, which was a common one during the Sassanid era. Apparently, that is the intention.

[5] So that on the Day of Fifty Thousand Years [Resurrection Day], when all particles of the body are reassembled and a person becomes whole, his body is not lessened.

Young boys should not eat dates religiously pledged to Omm al-Bani.

Young boys should not come close to the *samanu* pot, because Her Holiness Fatemeh is present.

A child who plays with fireworks will wet its bed at night.

If a boy sees food and is not given some, his manhood will burst.

If a boy smokes a clay-pipe, he will grow up to be a short man.

If a boy smokes opium, he will not grow a beard as a man.

When a child is born, it brings with it its own daily bread.

If a boy chews raw rice, he will become beardless.

It has been said that if a baby is given milk through a golden nipple of a bottle, he will become eloquent, become a sweetheart to the people, become physically manly, become immune to epilepsy, and will not be afraid in his sleep.[6]

"And if an unsheathed sword is placed by a seven-day-old child, that child shall be brave."[7]

A child who is ill-tempered and cries a lot should be taken and passed three times under the *Naqqarehkhaneh*[8] on Chaharshanbeh Suri evening, and also wheat should be put in a clay piggybank that is then smashed on the ground for pigeons to eat the wheat.

Lamcheh

This is an object for warding off the evil eye filled with musk, amber, and burnt wild rue, which they apply to the face and forehead of children.[9]

How to Immunize Children

After the mother takes the pulse of the baby, she pounds her own hand on the ground to send all the ailments and problems of the baby into the ground.

---

[6] *Nowruznameh*, p. 21.

[7] *Nowruznameh*, p. 38.

[8] *Naqqarehkhaneh* was a room above the door of Ark [a palace in Tehran], which has now been demolished.

[9] *Borhan Qate'*.

Double

It is a popular belief that when a child is born, a genie also comes into existence and accompanies that person. That genie is called the double.[10]

Breaking Eggs

To ward off the evil eye, with a piece of charcoal, they mark the top of an egg with the name of the child or the ailing person and the bottom of the egg with the name of the father of the child, then they name all the people who have seen the child one by one and mark the egg for each one, then in a piece of a dirty shirt of the child, they place the egg, a one-*shahi* coin, a little salt, and the charcoal, place it above the child's head, and once again repeat the names of the same people and squeeze the egg lightly. When the egg breaks upon the mention of a particular name, that person has had the evil eye. Then, they rub a little of the yolk of the egg on the soles and on the top of the head of the child and give the coin to a beggar.

Burning Wild Rue on a Charcoal Fire

When they show the baby for the first time, each person present gives a thread from his or her clothes to be burned along with wild rue to ward off the evil eye.

To ward off illness and the evil-eye,[11] they burn wild rue.[12] It is better to do this close to sunset. A piece of cloth or a thread from the pants or dirt from the sole of the shoe of the person under suspicion is taken, and with a little wild rue, they circle them around the head of the child or ill person and say:

> *Wild rue and wild rue seed*
> *Wild rue thirty-three seeds*

---

[10] *Borhan Qate'*.

[11] A newborn baby must be protected from the evil eye of religiously unclean people. (*Denkard*, 8-31-22.)

[12] "(7) And when they place the scent over fire and the wind carries that scent, up to the point where the scent reaches, one thousand times one thousand demons and lies are eliminated, scattered, and lessened, as are just as many sorcerers and demons and fairies. (8) And when there is a fire inside the house and they ignite it at midnight, one thousand demons are eliminated and twice as many sorcerers and fairies." (*Sad Dar Bundehesh*, p. 84)

From relatives and strangers
Whoever goes out through the gate
Whoever comes in through the gate
Let the eyes of the jealous and envious go blind
Born on a Saturday, born on a Sunday,
            born on a Monday... born on a Friday
Who planted it? The Prophet.
Who picked it? Fatemeh.
For whom did they burn it?
For Imam Hasan and Imam Hoseyn.
For sake of the King of Men
Turn away pain and calamity
Or they say:
Wild rue and wild rue
Our Prophet liked it
Ali planted it
Fatemeh picked it
For Hoseyn and Hasan
Born on Saturday, born on Sunday, born on Monday... born on Friday, under the ground, on the ground, black eyes, blue eyes, green eyes, hazel eyes, whoever has seen or not seen, the neighbor to the left, the neighbor to the right, in the front and in the back, may the eyes of the jealous and jealousy burst.

Haunted Child

It is believed that a child who has seizures, or is possessed by "Shadow,"[13] has been switched with a child of "our betters" [the jinn]. They put makeup on the child and place it in the corner of some ruins in order for "our betters" to take away their child and return the one they have switched.

---

[13] "They have said that Shadow is the name of a demon, and the jinn are also called Shadow. The reason for this name is that when a person becomes crazy, they said that the jinn have cast a shadow over him; in other words, they have altered him, and hence they called him possessed by 'Shadow.'" *Anjomanara Dictionary.*

On Teething

The child whose upper teeth emerge first is a bad omen. To ward off the bad omen, they drop him from a low roof into a chador.

How to Increase Breast Milk

When a wet nurse's milk is reduced, they sit facing the same direction as the Qibla and pound *ash-e reshteh* with a hundred dinars worth of milk in a mortar and feed it to her.

What to Do with Foreskin

In Rasht, it is common to skewer the foreskin of a child after circumcision with a pomegranate tree branch and hang it over the head of the circumcised child for seven days.

Eye Cure

For aching eyes, they make a gold or silver eye and send it to the shrine of the offspring of an imam.

Religious Pledge in Order to Have a Boy

A religious pledge is made that if the baby is a boy, they will not cut his hair for seven years, and after that period, they cut his hair and weigh it, then use as much gold as the weight of his hair to make a yoke or a dervish's alms bowl and send it to the shrine of the offspring of an imam.

Aqiqeh

A person whose sons do not survive makes a religious pledge to prepare an *aqiqeh* sheep, which means that a two-year-old sheep is slaughtered in a basement so it cannot see the sky. Then it is cooked whole in a large pot without any spices or salt. The meat of it must be eaten by religiously clean people, but its bones should not be thrown away. The bones should be collected and buried in the ground in the same basement.[14]

---

[14] Gathering and taking care of bones is found in common people's traditional stories, such as the son who was killed by his mother who served his flesh to her husband, and the son's sister gathered his bones and the son turned into a nightingale:

I am the wandering nightingale

When Possessed by the Jinn

If a child is possessed by the jinn, the child's mother and a girl must put their backs together and the child must pass through their legs, and then they must pass the child three times through the shoulder strap of a rifle.

Gurza

Gurza [born in a grave] refers to a child whose pregnant mother has died and the child is born in her grave. When this happens, they place the pregnant woman who has died in a grave and install a tube to let the air in from outside the grave until the child is born and they can hear its voice. Then they take the child out of the grave and raise it.

Fake Witchcraft

In Mazandaran, it is believed that bones grow in the throat of the infant of five or six months of age. To remove the bone, there are old women in a Wednesday market who, with sleight of hand, pretend to remove a bone, which they have hidden between their fingers, from the mouth of the child.

Ali Mowjud

In using scare tactics to stop a child from doing something, they say, "We will give you to Ali Mowjud." Ali Mowjud is supposed to be a dervish who takes children, impales them with four nails, lights an oil burner under them, and extracts their oil.

Wandering over hill and dale
My cruel papa slayed me
My mean step-mama ate me
And my kind sister washed my bones
Seven times with rose cologne
And buried them under the roses

Also, in the following idiom: "Even if they eat the flesh, they do not throw away the bones."

4

Various Beliefs and Ceremonies

Traveling

When someone is going to travel, they place on a tray a mirror, a plate of flour, and a bowl of water with a green leaf floating on top. After passing the traveler through the Yasin Ring and under a copy of the Koran, he must look in the mirror and put his finger in the flour, and then place it on his forehead. Upon his departure, they sprinkle the ground with the water.[1] Water and mirror symbolize light, and flour symbolizes blessing.

Three days or seven days after the traveler's departure, they cook *ash-e posht-e pa* [seeing-off soup], which is the same as *ash-e reshteh.*

If someone has a close relative traveling and has no news of him, on a Friday eve, he should go to an old well outside the city and call his name into the well. If he hears laughter from the well, the traveler is alive, and if he hears crying, he is dead.

When a traveler returns, a sheep is sacrificed before his feet.

Sisterhood

When two women want to take a vow of sisterhood, without seeing each other, a credible woman trusted by both, who is known as "green footed," must make a wax doll, place it in the middle of a tray full of sweets, and the woman who wishes to be

---

[1] (1) In olden times, when someone set out to travel less than twelve *parasang*s, they would consecrate a sacred cake to ensure that no harm would happen on that journey and affairs would be favorable to him and business would thrive. (2) And it is obligatory for everyone that when they want to travel they must consecrate the sacred cake. *Sad Dar*, chapter 53, p. 38.

the sister should send the tray to the other. If the other woman places a black chador on the doll, it means she rejects such a vow, and if she places a necklace around its neck and tips the messenger, both sides consent to become sisters.

Taking vows of sisterhood must be on the Feast of Ghadir, and in a shrine of an offspring of an imam. Drinking sherbet and playing the tambourine is mandatory.

One of the women says, "For the sake of the King of Kheybar."

The other answers, "Oh God, grant us our request and accept it."

Then they mention their own names and bear witness. The requirement for it consists of twelve handkerchiefs, which they tie in various forms, each of which has it specific name. Then they send them to each other as gifts, as stated in *Kolsum Naneh*.[2]

Midwifing for the Jinn
"Those better than us" [the jinn] need human midwives, and they take them with their eyes covered. When they take the midwife back, instead of money, they pay her with a fistful of onion skins. If the onion skins are placed under a carpet, every morning there will be a gold coin there; but if anyone is told about it, it will not work anymore.

Wish Dress
On the 27th of the month of Ramazan, which is the day Ibn Moljam was killed, women put on makeup with rouge and white powder, buy cloth with money they have panhandled, and in a mosque, sew a "wish dress" between two sets of prayers. When they sew this dress with the intention of recovery from illness, finding a good husband, or having children, their wish will be granted.

Finding a Husband
To bring good luck to a girl in finding a husband, they take her to a Jewish bathhouse.

---

[2] *Kolsum Naneh*, pp. 24, 25, 26.

After wedding vow ceremonies, if they seat a girl where the bride had been sitting, it brings good luck for her and she will soon find a husband.

To bring good luck in finding a husband to a girl, they stuff her chador in the intestines of a sheep.

Gift for Notables

In the city of Bam in Kerman province, when an important person entered the city, they would sacrifice the inner core of a male date palm tree by cutting off the growing bud of the tree, then they would take out the heart of palm, a coagulated sweet liquid in the inner core of the tree, and send it as a gift to that person.

Animal Sacrifice

The sheep which is chosen for this purpose must be wholesome and healthy. It is mandatory to lay it in the direction of the Qibla and put rock candy in its mouth and then take it out, because that rock candy is then considered blessed. They should remove the sheep's blood and liver using a black cloth to prevent the sky from seeing it. Such a sheep has many beneficial properties. For instance, its eyes are used to make charms to ward off the evil eye, and it is popularly believed that on the Fifty-Thousand-Year-Long Day [Resurrection Day], the sheep will volunteer to carry its killers on its back over the Serat Bridge.

Viewing the Moon

For each Islamic lunar month, specific things must be viewed. As the poet says:

> *Moharram is gold, and Safar is mirror*
> *First Rabi' is water, Second Rabi' is sheep*
> *First Jamadi is white silver*
> *Second Jamadi a respected person*
> *Rajab is a book, and Sha'ban is a flower*
> *The month of fasting is the*
> *   Sword of the World Conqueror*
> *Shavval is grass, and Ziqa'deh is a child*
> *Zihajjeh is the beautiful face of the beloved*[3]

---

[3] *Nesab*, published in Berlin, p. 56.

At the time of viewing the crest of the moon, on the whole, viewing an old man, water, a white horse, grass, a sword, and turquoise is good, and this poem is recited:

Oh Lord of the skies and the earth
With these six things I do need help
Wisdom, action, generosity
Faith, welfare, and health

To Rain or Not to Rain

In the villages of Khorasan province, to get rain, they usually make a doll's head on the top of a stick, dress it up, and then sing:

Rainbow, make the rain come
Endlessly make the rain come

To stop a downpour, they mention the names of seven bald persons, tie a knot on a string in the name of each, and hang it in the courtyard of the house, facing the same direction as the Qibla, or they draw an imaginary design of "Ya Ali" toward the sky with fingers, or they hang an inherited spoon upside down under the sky, or they write forty "Qs" on a piece of paper and hang it in the same direction as the Qibla.

Mohreh-ye Mar [Snakestone]

To get snakestones, when snakes mate, the person who volunteers to get the stones must be wearing blue pants. As soon as he sees the snakes, he must take off his pants and toss them on the snakes and run long enough to pass over seven streams of water. Then he should return and look for the stones. To test it, if a person has authentic snakestones, when he goes to a flatbread bakery, the bread will separate from the walls of the clay bread oven and fall down.

To Find a Thief

They bring a candelabra, hookah, or some sort of cover and write the names of the four archangels on them. Then write the names of the people they suspect separately on small pieces of paper and think of what is intended. Then two people remove the cover with the tip of their fingers and recite the "Yasin" chapter of the Koran. If the cover turns, the person whose name they have placed on the cover is the thief.[4]

Chelleh Neshastan [Seclusion for 40 Days]

There is a place in old mosques known as *chellehkhaneh*, which consists of small, dark, labyrinthine alcoves. The person who wants to go into seclusion in order to communicate with the jinn or fairies undergoes mortification of the flesh by going into the *chellehkhaneh*, drawing a line around himself, sitting in that circle, and consistently reducing the amount of his food intake, which is almonds or walnuts, by eating forty almonds on the first day, thirty-nine almonds on the second day, thirty-eight almonds on the third day, and so on, until the last day, the fortieth day, when his food will be only one almond, and the ghosts and evil spirits will appear to him.

To summon the absent person, they recite:

> *Alesoon-o belesoon*
> *Bring (so-and-so) real soon*
> *If he is sitting, make him stand*
> *If he is standing, make him run*
> *Pepper and peppercorns*
> *Bring him back to our home*

How to Extract More Oil

When they want to make homemade almond oil, in order to increase the amount of oil, women talk about the abundant flow of liquids. For instance, they say, "They killed someone in the alleyway. You can't imagine how much blood there was." Or they say, "There was a flood and so much water that it destroyed the houses." And as they say these things, they squeeze out the oil of the almond pulp.

To Prevent Tallness

If they want someone not to get tall, they make him stand against a wall, and a Hajj pilgrim who has traveled over a body of water pounds a nail above that person's head on the wall.

---

[4] In *Hajji Baba*, there is a detailed account of finding inherited money by means of witchcraft and sorcery.

Confining the Aleppo Boil

If they want to prevent an Aleppo boil from getting bigger, a Hajj pilgrim must draw a circle around it.

Getting Rid of the Ominousness of Safar

In the village of Jandaq, on the last Wednesday of the lunar month of Safar, they shoot a gun; then they bring a pitcher of water, set fire to a small bundle of brushwood, take the fire and water to the roof, and recite:

Off with calamity, off with fate
Off from our house and don't be late

Then they toss the fire and water down from the roof.

Love and Hate

In Azerbaijan, to plant love or hatred in someone's heart, commonly they mix yogurt and camphor, take it to a graveyard, pour it on a coffin, and say, "Plant love for me in so-and-so's eart" or "Make so-and-so have ill luck with so-and-so."

Witchcraft with Cockroaches

To bring bad luck to someone, they tie the backs of two cockroaches with blue thread, recite a prayer three times, and then bury them.

Goat-Leg Tossing

"They blow a charm on the leg of a goat and hide it somewhere in the alleyway. Goats gather there and butchers grab and kill them."[5]

New Clothes

When they put on new clothes, for good luck they say:

Happiness and wellbeing
Hope to wear it to a wedding

Channeling

To capture the jinn and fairies and communicate with spirits, they need to recite the Koranic verse "Qol uhay" [of the "al-Jinn" surah] one night continuously until morning.

---

[5] *Anjomanara Dictionary.*

Summoning the Prophet Khezr

The woman who undertakes this responsibility must be postmenopausal. First, for forty days early in the morning while everyone else is asleep, she must sweep and sprinkle water in the alleyway in front of the house door; and for twenty days, she must perform the *hajat* [need] prayers by the house door. On the fortieth day, at the crack of dawn, when she goes outside and is engaged in praying, suddenly she will see Khezr dressed as a shepherd, or a peddler, or a quilt and mattress maker, or a seyyed, or an old man with a white beard, and at that time she conveys to him what the person who hired her has in mind, and she will be inspired in her sleep, and the need will be fulfilled.

5

Conventions Regarding Ailments

Hunger Disease

A person who suffers from hunger disease has an owl in his stomach, and whatever he eats is food for the owl and does not nourish the patient. To treat it, the patient needs to go hungry for several days. Then his arms and legs must be tied together tightly, and aromatic and tasty food must be placed in his room in order for the owl to smell them and come out of the patient's stomach for the patient to be cured.[1]

To Cure a Head Cold

When someone catches a head cold, to cure it, he must take a bite of an onion and toss the onion on the roof of a neighbor's house, or he must ask someone jokingly, "Does a goat climb a mountain better, or a thief?" Regardless of whether the person who is asked answers "goat" or "thief," the affected person must respond, "Steal my head cold."

Eye Cure

When a white spot appears on the pupil of the eye or a black spot on the white part, the person must recite a prayer and blow on rice before soaking it.

For treating a sty in the corner of the eye, go to the bank of a river early in the morning and recite the following verses:

Dung, I say hello to you

---

[1] This myth and its treatment stems from common people's mispronunciation of *ju'* [hunger] as *jogh*, which is a mispronunciation of *joghd* [owl]. Hence, based on all this knowledge, they issue such a prescription for the poor patient.

As a slave, I am willing to serve you
Yet, if you do not cure my eye
My wish for you is to perish and die

For Quicker Recovery

If a person's illness is prolonged, a woman who has a husband looks for seven houses in which one girl there is named Fatemeh and asks for a couple of spoonsful of flour from each house. Then she takes some castor oil, goes to an intersection, makes dough out of the flour, which is known as "Fatemeh's flour," makes dough balls out of the dough, makes a fire, heats the oil on fire in a pan, browns the dough balls in heated oil, then runs a string through the browned dough balls, and in her heart resolves that she will not pull the string out of the balls before the ailing person is cured. Then she brings an unbaked clay brick, sprinkles salt on three corners of the brick, places three of the browned dough balls on the fourth corner of the brick, roasts some wild rue on the middle of the brick, places the brick at the intersection, hammers a nail on a wall above the brick, and hangs the string of browned dough balls on the nail. All this must be done on a Wednesday eve.

Chaharshanbeh-Suri Unbaked Clay Brick

For an ailing person, on a Wednesday eve, they bring an unbaked clay brick, light nine candles or wicks saturated with oil on the four corners of the brick, then they place on it a small coin, a little charcoal, wild rue, and spices. Then they take it to an intersection. However, the person who carries it must not turn around and look behind him or her.

They place musk, saffron, and a lit candle above the head of an ailing person, then pat the ailing person on the back and say, "May your pain and ailment go to the desert, go to the sea."

Evil Eye Cure

To eliminate the effects of the evil eye, they take the ailing person out of the city through the city gate.

Remedy with Neighbors' Help

In Jandaq, when a child becomes very ill, a woman dresses in white, picks up a *cheshmchin* (special knife), and a basket with her other hand. If the patient is male, she wears his hat, and if it is a female, she puts on that person's clothes, and then goes to other people's houses. She boils all the medicine and food that the people give her and feeds it to the patient. If they give her cloth, she makes a forty-piece dress and puts it on the sick child.

Treating Fevers and Shivers

For the treatment of a person who suffers from light intermittent fever (in other words, he has a fever once every three days), a married woman looks for three houses in each of which one wife of the man of the house has died, one wife he has divorced, and another wife is still in that house. Near sunset, the woman goes to each house without being recognized and says, "You have one wife who is dead, one whom you divorced, and one who lives in the house. What is the cure for intermittent fever?" Involuntarily, each man says something. No matter what they say, in the morning, the woman goes and finds whatever the men have said and gives them to the patient.

For a person who develops a fever at night, close to sunset, a woman in the same way looks for three houses in which a man has two wives. She goes to each and asks, "Man with two wives, what is the cure for night fever?" Each man answers involuntarily. Whatever each says they should give it to the patient.

If someone has severe shivers, whenever he starts to shiver, they bring a saddle of a black donkey and place it on his bedding, with the intention of transferring his shivers to the donkey.

To stop intermittent fever, they seat the patient on the edge of some stairs and, without warning, throw an earthen water jug above his head. From the sound of the breaking of the water jug, intermittent fever is frightened and leaps away. Or they slap the patient without warning.

Wild Rue to the Rescue

If the diagnosis is that someone has gotten sick due to the evil eye, they burn some wild rue and alum while concentrating on the evil eye. Then, from the burned remains, they mark seven places on his body.

6

For the Fulfillment of Wishes

In Kerman, people believe that an ailing person or a person who is facing a problem should ask his or her double or shadow for help, because they believe that the reason for bad incidents is intemperance and harming "those better than us" [the jinn]. If the ailing person is wealthy, they serve a banquet of greens on a supper cloth; and if he is poor, he is treated with "good scent." The necessity of the banquet on a supper cloth must be approved by the fortuneteller.

Good Scent

Near sunset, an old, experienced, trusted woman burns wild rue and frankincense and sets brushwood on fire. Then the ailing person jumps over it. If he is too feeble, others carry him over the fire.

Banquet of Greens on the Supper Cloth

In Kerman, there is a mountain they call "Tandorostan," and the common people believe that "those better than us" assemble there. They find an experienced old woman, who can be Zoroastrian. In other cities, they do this alongside a waterway, and the requirement is that there should be no one around the area.

The sponsor of the banquet of greens must absolutely obey the old woman. This supper cloth includes all the ingredients of the *Haft Sin* in addition to a variety of foods, and they must make sure that everything is clean and nice. It must in particular include *komaj* bread, *samanu*, a saltshaker, and an oil lamp or a candle.

The old woman sits alone at the head of the supper cloth and makes a request of the Daughter of the King of Fairies to bring health to the patient or grant the wish of the person. After the performance of these special ceremonies, if a black cat or a black pigeon comes to the supper cloth, the fulfillment of the wish is certain, because the Daughter of the King of Fairies might have turned herself into that shape [of the cat or pigeon], or the Daughter of the King of Fairies might be eating something from the supper cloth and putting her finger in the salt; otherwise, the ceremonies must be repeated.

Problem-Solving Mixed Nuts

To fulfill a wish and to ward off calamity, once a month, up to seven times, problem-solving mixed nuts [*ajil-e mosh-kelgosha*] must be bought, and the story of those mixed nuts also must be told. In the first month, they need to tie 100 dinars in the corner of a handkerchief and hand it to the nut seller without uttering a word. The nut seller knows what is requested and hands over the nuts. Problem-solving mixed nuts consist of seven ingredients—dates, pistachios, hazelnuts, almonds, roasted chickpeas, raisins, and dried mulberries—which should be divided among seven people.

The Story of Problem-Solving Mixed Nuts

Dear one, let me tell you, dear sir. Once upon a time, there was a poor thorn digger who was in dire straits. He had nothing. One day, he went to the desert to dig thorns. He saw a horseman. The horseman said, "Keep an eye on my horse, I will be right back." When he came back, he handed the man a fistful of pebbles from the desert. He then got on his horse and left. At sunset, when the thorn digger went back home, he was very depressed. He tossed the pebbles in the corner of the backroom closet and said, "I'll leave them here for the kids to play with." Then he went to bed to sleep. In the middle of the night, his wife got up and went to the cradle to nurse the baby. She noticed that there was a light in the backroom closet. She called her husband and asked, "What are these?" Then they figured out that the pebbles were worth a great deal. In the morning, he took a few of them to the bazaar and sold them and spent the money on buying new clothes for his children. He became quite rich.[1] Little by little, he

---

[1] Both the speaker and the audience know that, obviously, the horseman was Ali, and the pebbles blessed by his hand had turned to night-

became an important merchant. He set out to travel and used his money for trade. He told his wife, "While I'm gone, every month, buy one hundred dinars worth of problem-solving mixed nuts and give them away." He left. His wife had become friends with the wife of the king. They went to the public bathhouse together. After a while, when she went to the bathhouse with the wife of the king, one month she forgot to buy problem-solving mixed nuts. This time, when she went to the bathhouse, the sachet of the wife of the king got lost. They started a search to find out who had stolen it. They blamed it on the thorn digger's wife. They confiscated all the possessions of the woman and took them to the king's house. They arrested the woman and put her in jail. When the merchant returned from his travels, he went home to find that his house was in ruins and his wife and children were missing. The news of his arrival reached the private quarters of the king, and the merchant was also arrested and jailed. In the middle of the night while he was sleeping, the horseman came and kicked him lightly with the tip of his toe and said, "Inner blind man! Didn't I tell you to buy 100 dinars worth of problem-solving mixed nuts? There are 100 dinars under your shackle. Take it and buy problem-solving mixed nuts." The horseman disappeared and the prisoner woke up. He got up and went to the gate of the prison and asked a young man to take the 100 dinars and buy problem-solving mixed nuts for him. The young man said, "I have a wedding to go to; I don't have time to buy nuts for you." The merchant said, "I hope your wedding becomes a funeral." Another young man showed up and the merchant asked him to buy problem-solving mixed nuts for him. The young man said, "One of my kinfolk is sick and is about to die. I'm going to buy lotus powder and camphor for his burial." The merchant said, "I hope to God your relative recovers." The young man went and bought problem-solving mixed nuts for him, gave it away as charity, and also told the story of the nuts. Back in the king's house, the king's wife took her clothes off and went to the reflecting pool to bathe. She suddenly saw that a

---

glowing pearls. Problem solving is a specific attribute of Ali, whose problem-solving hand is well known:

Ali's hand is the hand of God, if you understand
No other hand solves problems as does God's hand

crow was holding her sachet in its beak and dropped it on her clothes. The king's wife said regretfully, "Oh God! Why did I do what I did and jailed these people for no reason?" The imprisoned couple were released from jail and their property was returned to them. As for the two young men who had passed by the prison gate, the first one went home and found that the bride had died, and the second one saw that his dying relative had recovered. May God solve your problem in the same way that He solved those people's problems.

Bibi Sehshanbeh Banquet at the Supper Cloth

This banquet at the supper cloth is spread on the last Tuesday of the lunar month of Sha'ban. The content consists of *kachi*, the ingredients of which have not been exposed to the sky and which has not been sweetened, since the sweetening syrup is served separately; unleavened bread; *kharbozeh* melon, if in season (otherwise, its seeds); dates; *qavut*; problem-solving mixed nuts; *ash-e reshteh*; an earthen jug; goat cheese; fresh green herbs; and so on, and the content must be purchased with panhandled money.

The owner of the house fasts. The women who sit around the supper cloth stick their fingers into the *kachi*, hold their hands in the air, and one of them tells a long story, a summary of which is as follows:

"There was a girl who had a stepmother. The stepmother harassed her a lot, and every day made her take her sheep to the desert to graze. One day, the sheep got lost. Fearing her stepmother, the girl cried and wailed and then made a religious pledge that if she could find the sheep, she would give a Bibi Sehshanbeh banquet at the supper cloth with panhandled money. As fate would have it, the sheep was found. By chance, the son of the king had come to hunt and saw her and fell in love with her head over heels and took her with him. The girl was in the private quarters of the king's house and could not organize the banquet at the supper cloth with panhandled money. She closed the doors of the room and panhandled the flour and the oil from the wall shelf. She said to the wall shelf, 'Aunty, dear. To please God, give me flour, give me oil.' She also asked for everything else. Then she took them to the backroom closet and started to cook *kachi*. By accident, her mother-in-law saw her. She went to

her son and said, 'You married a beggar for a wife and dishon-
ored us. She is just a lowlife and is used to panhandling. With all
the good food here, she panhandles from the wall shelf.'

"The king's son was outraged. As soon as he saw his wife
beside the cooking pot, he kicked the pot and all the *kachi* spilled
out, and two drops of it fell on his cotton shoes. Then the king's
son went hunting with two sons of the vizier. He had placed two
kharbozeh melons in his saddlebag. On the way, the vizier's sons
got lost. At lunchtime, when he looked into the saddlebag, he
saw that the two *kharbozeh* melons had turned into the two heads
of the vizier's sons and that the two drops of *kachi* had turned
into two drops of blood on his cotton shoes. His father was certain that he had killed the vizier's sons and thus put him in prison. From the prison, the king's son sent a message to his mother
and asked her to ask the girl about the *kachi*. The girl explained
about the religious pledge and cooked *kachi* again. The vizier's
sons were found, and the king released his son from prison."

Then those present suck on the finger which they had
dipped into *kachi*.

Fatemeh Zahra Banquet at the Supper Cloth

A woman who wants to perform this ritual must be religiously clean, not menstruating. This banquet is for eliminating
distress, debt, and illness, or with the intention of wishing to go
on pilgrimage, or other reasons. Meditating, the woman reflects,
"Oh Fatemeh Zahra! I plead to you in my need to rid me of this
problem."

These banquets at the supper cloth must be spread on a
Thursday, on a Friday eve, and repeated on three Friday eves.
For the first one, they must cultivate seven-and-a-half *sir*s of
pure flour in a green cloth bag and hang it on the door latch of
the room in order for the person making the religious pledge to
pass under the flour. (The second time, eight *sir*s, and the third
time, ten-and-a-half *sir*s); and in the morning, they use that flour
in a dark place that is not exposed to the sky to make *kachi* with
some oil and sweet substance. Then they pour it into a bowl and
cover it with a white cloth without touching it. Other ingredients
of the banquet at the supper cloth are as follows: sweets, sweet
mixed nuts, unleavened bread, sherbet, bread, fresh green herbs,
fruits, a fruit which is uncut (*kharbozeh* melon or watermelon),

and so on. At noon, all those who have been invited gather around the supper cloth. Then a narrator of stories of religious martyrs recites the stories of the martyrdom of the "Five Martyrs" [the Prophet Mohammad, his daughter Fatemeh, her husband Ali, and their sons Hasan and Hoseyn]. Then they remove the cover from the pot of *kachi*, which now has the mark of the finger of Fatemeh, and everyone eats some of the *kachi*, which has been blessed. They also divide the other foods among themselves. Men must not eat this *kachi*; and every woman who eats it must not be menstruating. The second banquet at the supper cloth is also done in the same way. However, they refrain from doing a third banquet at the supper cloth as a surety, until their wish has been fulfilled.[2]

Adjournment Ritual of the Commander of the Faithful, Ali
This ritual has its own special prayers, which are recited on four Friday eves; and prior to the prayers, the following verses are recited:

O Lord of both worlds, open the gate
O Commander of the Faithful, intervene in my fate
A problem in my affairs, it still lingers
Solve it on the hand of God with your two fingers

This prayer takes two to three hours, and after reciting various verses and chants, they lose their natural state of being and enter a celestial world. On the fourth Friday eve, when they beseech His Holiness for help, he is manifested in front of them riding a horse and carrying a sword. The persons who are performing the ritual involuntarily whirl around themselves on their toes while standing and come in front of His Holiness, make their requests, and then collapse on the ground and become unconscious. The result is revealed to them in their dream.

---

[2] There are also other banquets at the supper cloth, such as Bibi Hur and Bibi Nur, which I have disregarded here since they are all more or less similar.

7

Dreams

Keeping socks above one's head at night causes nightmares.

A person who dreams that he or she is dead will have a longer life.

If a person dreams of seeing God, he is an infidel.

If there are trousers above the head at night and the person has a bad dream, such a dream has no interpretation.

If one dreams that someone has gifted another with a copy of the Koran, the recipient of the gift will have a son.

Women's dreams are in reverse.

If a person sleeps facing a church, he will have nightmares.

If a pregnant woman dreams of seeing a sword, she will give birth to a boy.[1]

If a pregnant woman dreams of seeing a pearl, she will give birth to a girl.

If a person dreams about a horse, his or her wish will be fulfilled.

If a person goes to the bathhouse in his or her dream, he or she will go on pilgrimage.

If a dead person gives something to someone in that person's dream, that person will have a longer life, and if the dead person takes something from him, it is ominous.

Kissing in a dream will bring about separation.

A person who sees birds and fish in a dream, his wish will be fulfilled.[2]

If a person dreams of falling into a well, he will die.

---

[1] This concurs with S. Freud's interpretation.

[2] *If you see birds and fish in your dream*
You shall not die before becoming a king

If a person dreams of climbing heights, his affairs will improve.

If a person dreams of falling into an outhouse pit, he will find a lot of money.

Dreaming of snakes indicates wealth.

If a person dreams of losing his teeth, he will die.

Cows and calves in dreams are enemies.

Dreaming of seeing the moon will bring good news.

8

Death

On Friday eve, the dead are free and they come to the roofs of their houses. Hence, one should not speak behind their backs, and they should be remembered with good prayers.[1]

Every person has a star in the sky, which falls upon his death.

Whenever one sees a dead person in a dream, he should grab the big toe of the dead person to have that dead person tell him about the next world.

If a person has trouble sleeping at night and stays awake till morning, it means that one of his dead relatives is being tortured.

Early in the morning, dogs howl because they see the angel of death, Azrael; and in order for Azrael not come to the house, one shoe must be placed upside down.

Taking seven steps behind a coffin is religiously rewarded.[2]

---

[1] "(1) In revelation, it is stated that whenever it is the time of fathers, mothers, and children, or relatives, their spirits stand over the house and listen to hear their benediction. (2) Whenever they see the sacred feast and benediction, then ease, comfort, happiness, and joy will come to them. (3) And when they do not, they listen until evening prayers. (4) And when they lose hope by the time of evening prayers, they are hopeful up until midnight. (5) And when they do not receive prayers and benediction, they despair and say, 'O Creator, Ahura Mazda! They do not know that we are as we are, that it is necessary for them to come into this world, and in this world no one will be granted exoneration. Others need benediction, not that we need them. However, since they do not observe the sacred feast and do not offer benedictions for us, when calamity afflicts them, we cannot prevent it.' (6) They say this and once again go back to their own place." *Bundehesh,* p. 161.

Also see *Sad Dar Nasr,* in chapter 13, p. 12; in chapter 37, p. 28; in *Bundehesh,* p. 124.

To get religious reward, every man who sees a coffin should go under it and carry it for seven steps, or if he is walking in the opposite direction, he should take seven steps in the direction the coffin is being carried.

A person who dies at night should be not be left alone, and candles must be lit beside his head.

They place a stone above the head of the dead so that when the two angels Nakir and Monkar come to question him, his head hits the stone, he sneezes, and he says, "Thank Allah, the Lord of two worlds," and in this way, the angels will know that the dead person is a Muslim. For this reason, one should become accustomed to saying this phrase, such that it becomes second nature.

When they take the dead out of the room, they place an unbaked mud-brick in his place with a piece of meat on top of it, and at night, a bowl of sherbet, a plate of halva, and a lit lamp[3] in that room, and take them to his grave in the morning.

When they take the dead out of the house, they carry browned flour (halva, in front of the corpse) with a sheep flank in front of the coffin.

On every Friday eve, dates should be given to the poor as charity on behalf of the dead.

At the time of death, the eyes and the mouth of the deceased must be closed. If the eyes are open, it becomes clear that the dead person cannot forego his or her love for this world.

If the dead person's face shows a smile, he is going to Paradise, and if he makes an ugly face, he is a sinner.

If a dead person has done good deeds, they bury him quickly.[4]

---

[2] "They had to walk behind a coffin as much as they can, since every step taken behind it was rewarded with three hundred *astir*s and each *astir* was four dirhams, such that three hundred *astir*s was one thousand and two hundred dirhams, and the reward for every step was several times that amount." *Sad Dar Nasr*, p. 12.

[3] "(10) And all three nights on the place where his soul has departed must be placed three lights as bright as day." *Bundehesh*, p. 110.

[4] And since they are always hasty in burying the dead, hence, it often happens that they place him in the grave because he had fainted or suffered a stroke, and then he becomes conscious and it would take a long time before he dies in the grave.

If the coffin moves easily and is light, the deceased person has done good deeds.

If a sick person dies of fever, his sins are forgiven.

If the water with which the dead has been washed is dumped in the courtyard of someone's house, he will suffer from homelessness and exile.

If a living person lies in a coffin, the coffin squeezes him.

If a child of less than seven years of age dies, he will go to Heaven.[5]

If a woman dies, after placing her in the grave, a relative who is religiously allowed to see her must uncover her face.

When they bury a dead person, they walk away seven steps and return to the grave, because the dead person is expecting them.

Eating the halva prepared for the funeral of an old person prolongs life; but one should not eat the halva prepared for the funeral of a young person who has died.

Those who are accustomed to dying their nails with henna will not be interrogated by the angels on their first night in the grave.

They place a copy of the Koran on the chest of the dead person. If they do not, Satan will enter the dead person's body.[6]

---

[5] "(1) When a child of seven years shall die, an order is necessary and it is requisite to perform the ritual for Sorush on account of it, and to consecrate the sacred cake of the fourth night. (2) For it says in revelation that the souls of children go with the souls of their fathers and mothers; if the father is fit for Heaven the child goes to Heaven with him, if he be fit for Hell it arrives in Hell; if the mother be fit for Heaven it reaches Heaven with her; if she be fit for Hell it reaches Hell with her. (3) Therefore, every time that they carry out the ritual for Sorush, the soul of that child becomes separated from the souls of its father and mother and goes to Heaven, and is imploring intercession for its father and mother in the presence of the sacred beings in that other world." *Sad Dar*, chapter 47, p. 36.

[6] There is a well-known story about a dead man who was taken to Nayebossaltaneh Mosque the night before his burial. A lame preacher who served as the custodian of the mosque was sitting next to the corpse reading the Koran. In the meantime, he sees the corpse in the coffin begin to wiggle and move. Frightened, he gets up and runs, limping, out of the room. The corpse also gets up and follows him. The preacher hits the corpse with the copy of the Koran in his hand and

The popular belief is that Jews put a fistful of roasted chickpeas in the pocket of the dead person and say:

When Ankar and Monkar come,
*   blow into their eye sockets*
But when Moses comes, put the chickpeas in his pocket
Grab the key to Paradise and jump inside

Jaridatayn

They place two sticks, *jaridatayn*, under the arms of the dead so that the dead can lean on them during the interrogation in the grave.[7]

Kaseh-ye al-Afv

The final bowl of water poured over the head of the dead by the mortician is called *kaseh-ye al-afv* [forgiveness bowl], on which the mortician blows and then pours it over the dead person's head.

Pressure of the Grave

When the grave puts pressure on the body, all the milk that the person has from his or her mother nursing comes out of his or her nose.

---

recites "In the name of God." The corpse collapses on the ground. A characteristic of this type of dead people whose body is entered by the jinn is that they cannot talk, but they are capable of everything else, and as soon as it is dawn, they die again. This description is not dissimilar to the beliefs of Europeans regarding vampires in the Middle Ages.

[7] *Jaridatayn* must be from the wet branches of trees such as willow, pomegranate, or fig trees. They are cut in a specific length. This is reminiscent of Zoroastrians' *barsam*.

9

Fortunetelling by Body Parts

A big head indicates wisdom and sagacity.[1]
A high forehead indicates wealth.
A short forehead indicates poverty and abject-
ness.[2]

A long beard is indicative of stupidity.

A sparse beard and blue eyes are indicative of roguery.

Tallness is indicative of idiocy.

Shortness is indicative of cleverness, wisdom, and cunning-
ness.[3]

If you pinch the palm of the hand, it is indicative of giving a
promise.

A blunt eye (that opens the way) means a guest is coming.

---

[1] Mazandarani saying: "The shepherd has big feet, and the king, a big
head."

[2] "Philosophers have said that a wide forehead on which there are no
lines, one that has no wrinkles and folds, is an indication of hostility,
stupidity... boasting and exaggeration; a thin, narrow forehead indicates
turpitude, misery, and abjectness; and an average forehead is indicative
of intelligence, knowledge, insightfulness, and prudence." *Akhlaq-e
Mohseni.*

[3] Notables have said: "A short wise man is better that an ignorant tall
man." Verse:

The messenger of God has been said to admit
That a tall person is of little wit.

"It has been mentioned in books of history that a short man asked for
justice in the presence of Nowshirvan and said, 'Someone has done
injustice to me.' Nowshirvan said, 'No one can do injustice to a short
man; rather, he would do injustice, and you are short.' The short man
replied, 'O King, the one who has done injustice to me is shorter than
me.' Nowshirvan smiled and restored justice to him." *Akhlaq-e
Mohseni*, p. 188.

The curse of a person the roof of whose mouth is black is effective.[4]

A person who uses his left hand to clip the fingernails of his right hand can make a living on his own.

If fingernail clippings are dropped underfoot, they will cause poverty. Rather, nail clippings should be placed at the base of the door, so that on the day that Dajjal [Anti-Christ] appears, they will grow like thorns and not allow the people in the house to leave.

If you drop hair from the head on the road, sparrows take it to make a nest, and the person whose hair was dropped will get vertigo.[5]

An extracted tooth must be given ablution three times, then placed in a shroud and buried in a hole in a wall.[6]

---

[4] *Zaqzaban* [blue tongue] alludes to people with black tongue. In other words, their curses are effective (*Borhan-e Qate'*).

"Sky mouth from above: If from the back of the teeth it is black about 2.5 inches, the horse is called *saq siyah* [blackness of the roof of the mouth], which is said to be very bad, especially for the one who owns it, even if it has a white vein." *Farasnameh* by Asadollah Khonsari.

[5] "(10) Whenever one throws one filament of hair and in his heart he intends not to catch it and to avoid a command, it is a sin, whether minor or major." *Sad Dar Bundehesh*, p. 81.

[6] The hiding of nails, hair, and teeth is to prevent enemy access to them, since one of the sorcery acts which is common today in the Jewish neighborhood is *envoûtement* [bewitchment]. For this act, the sorcerer makes a figurine out of wax, places the tooth, head hair, or nail of the enemy in the wax figurine, and after performing specific ceremonies, every part of the body of the figurine that he injures, that same part of the person whose nail or hair is used will become injured. This is also done by using a live mouse and by burying a candle in a graveyard.

It is stated in *Qesas al-Olama* that Mirza Mohammad Akhbari used bewitchment to bring the head of the Russian commander, Eshpokhtor (Tsitsianov), to Fathali Shah. A common saying is: "Do you think you have brought the head of Eshpokhtor?"

In the Avesta (chapter 17), it is emphasized that they must strive to take care of head hair and nails to prevent them from falling into the hands of (Yaduk) sorcerers.

"(1) When the nails are pared according to custom, it is necessary that they put the parings into a paper. (2) And it is further necessary to

A man's hairy chest is indicative of love for Ali.

One must not find fault with anyone's nose, because God has made it with His own hands.

When the tip of the nose hardens, it is the sign of adulthood.

If the tip of the nose itches, the person will go to a party.

If the soles of the feet itch, the person will travel far.

When the palm of the right hand itches, it should be rubbed on the head of the oldest son for that son to make a lot of money.

If the palm of the left hand itches, the person will spend a lot of money.

One sneeze is a signal for waiting. In response, they say, "May you have good health." To end the waiting, they must recite the salutation to the Prophet Mohammad and his family seven times. Two sneezes signal *jahd* [attempt], which means one must hurry. Whether healthy or sick, a person who sneezes will certainly live for at least three more days.[7]

---

take the Prayer of Protection inwardly, and to utter three 'Yatha Ahu Vairyo' mantras... (10) It is altogether necessary that they do not leave them unbroken, for they would come into use as weapons of wizards." *Sad Dar Nasr*, chapter 14, p. 13.

[7] Hadith: "Sneezing provides protection from death for up to three days." For this reason, after sneezing, one should thank God and say, "I thank Allah, the Lord of both worlds." The benefit of this is that when in the grave the interrogating angels, Nakir and Monkar, come to the grave and one's head hits the stone and that dead person sneezes, because he is accustomed to it, one would say, "I thank Allah, the Lord of both worlds," and it will become evident to Nakir and Monkar that he is a Muslim.

"(1) When a sneeze comes forth from anyone, it is requisite to recite one 'Yatha Ahu Vairyo' and one 'Ashem Vohu' mantra. (2) Because there is a fiend in our bodies, and she is an adversary who is connected with mankind, and strives so that she may make misfortune and sickness predominant over mankind. (3) And in our bodies there is a fire which they call a disposition—in Arabic they say *tabi'at*—and they call it the sneezing reflex. (4) It is connected with that fiend, and they wage warfare, and it keeps her away from the body of man. (5) Then, as the fire becomes successful over that fiend, and puts her to flight, a sneeze comes because that fiend comes out. (6) Afterwards, because it is necessary, they recite these inward prayers and perform the benediction of the fire, so that it may remain for a long period while thou art keeping this fiend defeated. (7) When another person hears the sneeze, it is

When a person hiccups, they accuse him of stealing, so that the fear would stop the hiccupping.

One must not yawn in front of anyone, because it will cause misfortune for the other person. To remedy it, they should pat the back of the person who has yawned and he must look up.

If someone yawns, two other people in the same house will also certainly yawn.[8]

The fluttering of the left eyelid brings happiness.

The fluttering of the right eyelid brings sadness and sorrow.[9]

If an eyelash falls out on the cheek, it means sudden death and must be removed immediately.

If someone bites his own tongue, people are talking behind his back at the same time.

If while talking, involuntarily someone's name is mentioned, that means that person has been thinking about the one who mentioned his name at the same time.

If a person looks cross-eyed at someone and at the same time a mouse goes from one hole to another, his eyes will stay crossed.

If a person kisses the back of the neck or the eyes of someone, he will lose that person's affection.

If the fingernails of one hand are clipped and those of the other hand are not clipped, that person will be attacked by a dog.

Having a mole on your hand, be glad
Indicates pilgrimage to Mashhad
Having a mole on your feet, hurrah
Indicates pilgrimage to Karbala
Having a mole upon your chest

---

likewise requisite for him to utter the said prayers, and to accomplish the benediction of that spirit." *Sad Dar*, chapter 7, p. 7.

[8] There is a popular story about a man who yawned and his wife also yawned. Because no one else was in the house, he went in search of the third person and found his wife's lover in the closet.

[9] "The fluttering of the upper right eyelid is indicative of happiness after sorrow, and of the left, the arrival of an absent person, and (the fluttering of the lower eyelid) of the right means sorrow and of the left, indicative of news one is hoping to receive, or of the right eyelid, illness, and of the left eyelid, happiness." *Jannat al-Kholud*.

Indicates repairing your clothes, at best
Having a mole upon your face
Is indicative of good grace

For common people, especially for roughnecks, a mustache used to be particularly important and prestigious, indicative of manliness and chivalry and indisputably deserving of respect.

10

Augury, Foretelling, Good Omen, Bad Omen

When the heels of shoes are clicked together, the owner will become wealthy.

If smoke moves toward someone, he is rich.

The first money earned from someone with an auspicious hand early in the morning, or the first of the month, or the first day of the year indicates that the person will be wealthy for the rest of the day, the month, or the year.

If the wooden downstem of a hookah falls into the water of the hookah, the smoker will receive money, provided he takes the stem out of the base, kisses the top of it, and then puts it back in place.

If a person unknowingly puts on his clothes inside out, he will receive money.

If the back of a man's clothes get folded, he will receive money.

If someone pats the back of a man and dust rises, that man is able to make a living for himself.

If three plates are lined up in a row, guests will be coming. If there is a small dish next to them, the guest will be accompanied by children.

If tea leaves float vertically in the tea glass, a guest will come.

If a bite of food falls out of the mouth, guests will be coming.

If a hookah makes noise and spreads sparks, guests will be coming.

If water says hello (while pouring it, the water splashes back and makes a noise), guests will be coming.

If an earthen jug of water condensates, guests will be coming.

61

If water or a bite of food makes a person gag, he will receive a souvenir.

If a glass of water topples, it implies brightness.

If a cigarette is lit only on one side, the smoker will find a good wife.

If the good fortune mirror of the bride breaks, either the bride or the groom will die.

Wives, houses, and horses can be good or bad omen.

If a woman passes by between two people, hurdles will appear in one's affairs.

If a married woman steals a supper cloth, her husband will die.

If a woman braids her hair in the hot water pool of a public bathhouse, she will have a co-wife.

If a girl wears her black chador inside out, she will find a good husband.

If a girl whose father is alive unbraids her hair at home, it is a bad omen.

Passing through a herd of sheep or a caravan of camels brings poverty.

Staying in a house of ill omen will cause illness, entanglement, or death.

A religiously unclean traveler in a car causes the breakdown of the car (will cause a flat tire).

Putting on trousers while standing up brings poverty.

If the clouds form the shape of a camel, there will be pestilence that year.

Any knot in the affairs that opens by itself is good and is a means for facilitating the affairs.

If cobwebs are as straight as strings, they indicate a forthcoming trip.

If a traveler encounters a red-haired woman as he is leaving the house, it is a bad omen.

If fireworks fall into the courtyard of a house, there will be a wedding in that house.

A comet can bring good or bad luck; it can be a good omen or a bad omen.

Crouching on a threshold will cause defamation. To counter it, spit on the door on the side you are on.

A man who puts on makeup will go to prison.

A black cloud brings a downpour and stops quickly, whereas rain from a gray cloud is persistent.[1]

If the blades of scissors are left open or opened and closed
rapidly, a quarrel will ensue.

If money or keys on a keychain are clinked, there will be a
quarrel.

Handing a pair of scissors to a person results in hatred for
that person.

If one shoe is left on the top of another, the owner will travel far.

Gifting a knife to someone will sever friendship.

A hat should not be placed upside down on the ground, because its owner will die.

Cutting paper and cloth into small pieces will cause poverty.

If a crystal or porcelain dish breaks, one should not get up-
set, because it is the result of fate and calamity.

Drinking water while lying on one's stomach will diminish
intellect.[2]

If several people are sitting together, they must not be
counted, because their number will diminish.

Singing in the outhouse causes madness.

Going into the outhouse without a head cover causes madness.

Singing into a vat causes madness.[3]

In backgammon, if the dice falls out of one's hand, it is an
indication of the loss of the game.

The accidental falling of the king while playing chess indicates checkmate.

Refraining from eating meat for forty days results in madness.

A cook who makes the food too salty wants a husband.

Showing humility at the supper cloth causes debt.

---

[1] *Fear not a black cloud or a man with a full beard*
Fear instead a white cloud and a man with a sparse beard.

[2] Example: A person was lying on his stomach drinking water from a
stream. Someone told him, "Don't drink water like that. Your intellect
will diminish." He asked, "What is intellect?" The man answered,
"Nothing. I wasn't talking to you."

[3] A vat improves one's voice. Idiom: "The fellow sings into a vat."

A person who tears bread into many small pieces at the supper cloth will have many children.

Yellow clothes can bring good or bad luck; but white, green, and black clothes bring good luck.

When the wood of clothing trunks, tables, and jewelry boxes dries up and makes a noise, it causes homelessness and exile.

If bath mittens are rubbed on the face, one will lose one's good reputation.

If a person uses someone else's comb to comb his or her hair, the relationship between them will cool down and the one whose comb is used will lose affection for the other.

If you steal food from a miser and eat it, you will never get sick.

Stealing something from a traveler's provisions for the trip will make the traveler return soon.

Money received from a miser should be used as capital for a thriving business to be always wealthy.

If someone writes a letter and does not cut off the bottom, his wife will die.

If you hit someone with a broom, that person's life will be shortened. To prevent it, the bristles of the broom must be broken.

If someone is hit with a hookah hose, he will become scrawny.[4]

A mason who builds a firepit stove will become a homeless exile.

If a cobbler makes two shoes the same size, his wife will die.

Reading *Amir Arsalan* and *One Thousand and One Nights* will result in becoming a homeless vagabond.

If one hits the underside of the top of a *korsi* (drumming), it will rain.

If a hunter gives the liver of the prey he has shot to a pregnant woman, his hands will be tied and he can no longer hunt.

"And in his *Book of Weapons*, Bahram has stated that when the sword is pulled out of the scabbard and it moans, it is a sign of shedding blood; and when the sword comes out of the scabbard by itself, it is an indication of war; and when an unsheathed

---

[4] Popular saying: "He is as thin as a hookah hose."

sword is placed beside a child for seven days, that child will grow up to become brave."[5]

"And there are four benefits from a man with a handsome face. The first is that it makes the day auspicious for the seer; the second is that it makes life pleasurable; the third is that it opens the way to chivalry and magnanimity; and the fourth is that it increases wealth and status."[6]

If a person orders his own grave to be built, his life will be prolonged.

If a person sponsors the building of a mosque and has it completed, he will soon die.[7]

---

[5] *Nowruznameh*, p. 38.

[6] *Nowruznameh*, pp. 71-72.

[7] For this reason, everyone who sponsors the building of a mosque leaves a part of it incomplete.

11

Hours, Times, Days

Seeing a coffin early in the morning is a good omen.
If the bride is taken to the groom's house on a Friday eve, her mother-in-law will die.

If a wife removes her facial hair by threading for three consecutive Fridays, her husband will divorce her.

If you whistle at night, you will be haunted by the jinn.

When sewing clothes, if someone is walking and the steps are light, the sewing will be finished quickly, and if the steps are heavy, sewing that garment will take a long time.

The word "halva" should not be mentioned at night.

If nails are clipped on a Saturday, debts will be paid, if on a Monday, you will get rich. Clipping nails on a Friday brings religious reward; on a Thursday, the inheritance of offspring will arrive.[1] Clipping nails at night causes weddings and mourning to be mingled.

If you light candles at forty pulpits on the eve of Ashura, any wish you have will be fulfilled.

Guests coming on a Friday eve bring goodness and blessing, and if they leave on that same eve, they take goodness and blessing with them.

In Isfahan, people believe that near the day of Ashura, the air becomes dusty and depressing.

The lunar month of Safar is ominous and, in particular, its thirteenth day is considered the most ominous.

---

[1] *As for shaving your head and clipping your nails, keep it at bay*
Specifically on Sunday and Tuesday, and also Saturday

The month of Safar is so ominous that out of 124,000 prophets, 120,000 of them have died in that month.

The first night you sleep in the courtyard for summer must be an even day. Odd days are a bad omen.

A person who sleeps in a public bathhouse or under a tree will become haunted by the jinn.

Going to the public bathhouse on a Sunday is a bad omen.

The gift of life of anyone who sneezes on the eve of the twenty-third day of the lunar month of Ramazan is renewed, and that person will live for at least another year.

When the month of Ramazan reaches the days that end with -*hom* (*nohom, dahom*) [ninth, tenth], it will end soon.

One should not visit anyone's house on a Sunday eve.

Wednesday eve belongs to Ayesheh.[2]

If hot water is sprinkled at night or fire is tossed and the name of God is not mentioned, the person doing so will become haunted by the jinn, because the sleeping children of "those better than us" have been hurt.[3]

On the eve of the fifteenth day of the lunar month of Sha'ban, if a person's shadow on the wall is headless, he will die by the following year.

You must not sweep at sunset, because the house will disappear.

Washing a man's clothes on a Friday will make him a panhandler.

If a female panhandler comes at noon, it is the devil; but if it is a male panhandler, he is an angel.

If a person uses a needle to sew on the day of the Feast of Ghadir, he will get the infection, whitlow finger.

---

[2] Proverb: "On Wednesday, someone has found money, while someone else has lost money."

[3] "First, at night do not pour outside toward the north any boiled herbal medicine and any stews, since the demon will get pregnant and the person who pours it must recite the 'Yatha Ahu Vairyo' mantra." *Shayest Nashayest*, 7, p. 128. Published by Tavadia.

"(1) It is not proper to pour away water at night, especially from the northern side, which would be the worst. (2) Therefore, if it becomes necessary in the end, it is required to recite one 'Yatha Ahu Vairyo' mantra, and once they make a light ready, to pour away the water gently." *Sad Dar*, chapter 30, p. 24.

If a person sews on the day of the Feast of Sacrifices, blades will pierce the feet of Hajj pilgrims in Mecca.

Saturday is onerous for traveling.[4]

On Sunday eve and Wednesday eve, one should not visit a sick person at sunset.

If you hear a sound at night in the darkness, it is the voice of your double.

On the first day of the month and the first day of the Persian New Year (Nowruz), all the lights in the house must be turned on.

Eating *reshteh polo* [a rice and noodles dish] on Nowruz eve helps in controlling one's affairs.

If you go to the public bathhouse on forty Tuesdays, you shall suffer madness.

In a dark basement or hallway at night, you must say "in the name of Allah," otherwise, you will be haunted by the jinn.

New clothes made or worn on a Tuesday will eventually burn.

Combing hair and looking into the mirror at night will cause distress.[5]

If a woman looks into a mirror at night, she will have a co-wife, unless she turns the mirror around a lamp three times.

A businessman does not sell on credit to his first customer of the day, but he gives a discount.

At sunset, you should not turn away a customer, but you should also not sell on credit.

If a person spends a Tuesday eve at a house in which some-one is sick, he must also stay there on a Sunday eve. The same is true regarding Tuesday eve and Thursday eve.

You should not take medicine, go to a doctor, or visit an ill person on the first day of the month.

"If the Baba Shoja'oddin Feast Day occurs on a Tuesday, Wednesday, or Friday of the first of the month, whoever dies in

---

[4] Idiom: "On Saturday, if even a stone rises from its place, it will go back to where it was."

[5] It is commonly believed that Joseph looked into a mirror at night and for that reason, he was in prison for seven years.
Do not look into the mirror at night
Do not darken your bright daylight.

that month should be buried along with a pair of his own shoes, which would prevent the death of any of his relatives."[6]

"On the eve or on the day of the twenty-seventh day of the month of Ramazan, light twelve wicks to have your wishes fulfilled."[7]

Do not sweep on Tuesdays and Wednesdays.

Sweeping on the first day of the month brings good luck.

If a person is in a house in which someone dies and he spends the night, he must stay there for seven consecutive nights.

The Yalda Night, or winter solstice, is the longest night in winter, and you must eat watermelons on that night.

It is bad omen to take water from someone else's house at night. You can, however, take some water to that house and sprinkle it, and then take water.

Those who go to a water well or a *qanat* at sunset will be haunted by the jinn.[8]

You must have *kuku* [an herb soufflé] on the supper cloth on the night before Nowruz, but on the evening after Nowruz, you must not have *kuku*, because mentioning its name will cause poverty.[9]

Early in the morning, when a person leaves his house, if he sees an empty dish in someone's hand, it is a sign of the absence of blessing.

On *Sham-e Ghariban* [Night of Lonely Strangers], the stove of the house must be turned off.

It is dangerous to travel in the month of Safar.

In the Small Chelleh of winter, after the winter solstice, Ahman tells Bahman, "I'll take care of everyone and everything."

At night, to know the next day's weather, people huff in front of a lamp. If the lamp turns red, it will be sunny, and if it turns white, it will be rainy.

"And I have quoted some of the effects and changes from the books of the people of Iran and the Egyptians. When the

---

[6] *Kolsum Naneh.*

[7] *Kolsum Naneh.*

[8] "Water drawn at sunset is unpleasant." *Shayest Nashayest.*

[9] *Kuku* [meaning: where is it, where is it?] is asking for what does not exist.

moon on the third or fourth night is limpid and clear, the next day the weather will be clear; and if on the night of the middle of the month, the moon is clear, the weather will be clear; and if it is red, it indicates much wind; and if it is black, it is the sign of precipitation; and if the sun at the time of its rise is clear, or before sunrise miscellaneous bits of cloud appear, or at the time of sunset, there is no cloud and it becomes cloudy after or before sunset, all these indicate a delay in rain... When sparrows make a great deal of noise in the trees, it indicates rain... When they take off the cooking pot from the stove tripod and there are many sparks at the bottom, or a hen scratches itself a great deal and makes a lot of noise, or a swallow flies around a whirlpool and makes a great deal of noise, or if a buffalo stands facing the west and does not place one leg fully on the ground, or a large number of wolves come to the village, or a mouse tosses out things it has saved from its hole, all these indicate rain, especially at the beginning and end of the month; and when there is pure red color around the moon, it is a sign for cold weather; and if two or three yellow or red rings appear around the moon, it is indicative of severe cold weather; and the great noise of flies inside the house and the jumping up from the ground of sheep in the pasture, and the lamp's light appearing as darkness, all these are signs of cold weather; and when the birds come down from the trees and float in water, it is the sign of cold weather and rain; and in the year when oak trees and pepper trees produce a great deal, the winter in that year will be long; and when a donkey stands facing the west, digging the ground with its foreleg and looking at the sky, it is indicative of a long winter."[10]

> When there is a halo around the moon, again
> > Yes, potentially it is proof of rain
> Whoever sees the halo of your face will weep in pain
> > When there is a halo around the moon, it is proof of rain

Kolukhandazan [Clod Throwers]

This is a festival celebrated by wine drinkers at the end of the month of Sha'ban, when they drink excessively, and it is also called *Sangandazan* [stone throwers].[11]

---

[10] *Falakossa'adeh*, p. 74.
[11] *Anjomanara* Dictionary.

12

General Guidelines

Water and salt are the dower of Fatemeh Zahra and must not be polluted or denied to anyone.[12]

The saliva of old women is nitric acid.

When drinking water, it must be given to the younger ones first. If acting on the contrary, on Judgment Day, the young one must be carried on your shoulders. Another saying states that if the younger person does not drink water first, the water will dry up at the source.

One should not drink water while standing, because it will go to the veins and vessels of the legs.

If water is placed on the supper cloth, Shemr will have access to it.[13]

One must not urinate in water, because it is the dower of Fatemeh.

If you pour a half-consumed glass of water on your hands, the corners of the fingers will develop whitlow. To remedy it, you must spit on a door latch and then rub the saliva on the back of your fingers.

Drinking a fistful of hot water from the pool in the public bathhouse is religiously recommended.

Splashing water on someone is a sign of lack of affection.

---

[12] (16) And it is a sin to vomit in water or to urinate in water. (17) It is a sin to spit in running water. (18) And it is a sin to vomit on fire or water. (19) And [it is a sin] to throw carrion into water or fire. *Sad Dar Bundehesh*, pp. 82, 148.

[13] Shemr is in the shape of a four-eyed dog who constantly runs after water, and from afar he sees a mirage but can never reach water, because he denied water to the family of Imam Hoseyn in Karbala.

Bread is bounty from God. It must not fall on the ground. If it does, you must pick it up and secure it in the crack of an outside wall.[14]

Fire melts the fat in wolves' eyes.

Constructing buildings prolongs life.

An old person is the blessing in the house.

If a woman is impolite to her husband, she will be religiously forbidden at his house.

A man should not sleep alone in a white room.

Every falling star is the life of a person that has extinguished.

For anyone who practices sorcery, its evil results will come back to that person, who will be engulfed in abomination.

Alchemy brings about abomination.

Sleeping alone, eating alone, and traveling alone is inauspicious.[15]

To go on pilgrimage, the imam must summon you.

You must not sweep when you have guests in the house.

Do not urinate on a green tree.

Do not throw stones at a green tree.

If you get a mole tattoo on the Feast of Ghadir, it will become a moon on Resurrection Day.

Eye ache belongs to Ali and toothache belongs to Omar.

Men should not eat *qavut* [mixture of sugar and roasted chickpea flour] at the supper cloth rituals of Bibi Hur and Bibi Nur.

The whiteness of a girl's neck has the scent of Paradise.

If the breaking-of-the-fast cannon is fired and someone has not broken his fast, the rewards of that fast will be taken away by Satan.

If a piece of wood makes a noise while burning, you should say "shoo," since it is the sound of a dog that has come from Hell to take away the fire.

---

[14] This is similar to Zoroastrian thinking on this subject.

[15] "(2) Before eating bread, they must first say thanks to Ohrmazd and be grateful for all the bounty and be ardent in eating bread. (3) Once they end eating bread, once again they thank Ohrmazd." *Sad Dar Bundehesh*, p. 131.

After reading the Koran, it should not be left open, since Satan will read it.

Excessive combing of one's beard will increase libido.

If putting on trousers while standing, your prayers will not be answered for three days.

Do not look at a guest's bites of food.

Sticking a bone from *khoresh* [meat sauce] into plain cooked rice is an insult to the cook.

After the departure of a traveler, one should not write a letter or have him followed.

Dinner must be eaten to break the mood of the evening.

When a person does good deeds, the angel on his right shoulder writes it down, and when he commits bad deeds, the angel on the left shoulder does.

When a person sees a new place, he must give away a black hen.

The number 13 is sinister.

If a person cuts off the edges of the bread, on Resurrection Day those edges will become snakes and wrap around his neck.

It is a sin to cut bread with a knife.

Do not burn the rind of *kharbozeh* melon, since Ali's name is written on it.

If the steps of the physician or visitor who visits a patient are light and good, the patient will recover soon, and if they are heavy, his condition will worsen.

Do not point an unloaded gun at anyone, because Satan might have loaded it.

Do not hand to anyone a jackknife that is open.

Invoking the name of Allah will make the jinn, the ghouls, and the devils flee.[16]

It is a sin not to finish the food and have leftovers.

Before having children, a wife should not leave the house with her husband.

A woman must turn on the light of her own house at sunset.

One must say hello to panhandlers, since one of them might be the Prophet Khezr, who has disguised himself as a beggar.

It is worthy of religious reward to throw bones on the roof.

---

[16] Idiom: "Money is a ghoul and I am the name of Allah."

On Resurrection Day, eyes move to the tops of heads and a father cannot even recognize his own son.

Close to Resurrection Day, the human race will become so small that an old woman can sit in the hose of a hookah and weave baskets.

The Serat Bridge is thinner than a hair and sharper than a sword.

Shemr's dagger is in a basement, and on Ashura day, blood drips from it.

Whatever exists on the land also exists in the sea.

God is capable of placing the entire word in an eggshell without the eggshell getting larger or the world getting smaller.

When the world comes to an end, it will become as flat as the palm of a hand, such that if they place an egg on this side of the world, it can be seen on the other side.

The world was created for the sake of The Five [the Prophet Mohammad, his daughter Fatemeh, her husband Ali, and their sons Hasan and Hoseyn].[17]

A person who commits suicide does not die. He will be crucified in the next word and will be suspended between the earth and the sky until the time for his natural death arrives, because life and death are at the command of God, not humans.

Seyyeds are paternal cousins.[18]

When several people are conversing and suddenly everyone becomes silent, this indicates that at that moment a treasure is passing by under the ground. According to another version, the angel of death, Azrael, is passing through.

We must constantly thank God and not criticize His work in order for His bounty to increase.

Upon thanking for bounty, that bounty will increase
Heathenism will remove the bounty from your reach

---

[17] (2) For it is declared in revelation that the creator Ohrmazd spoke to Zoroaster thus: "O Zoroaster! I have created no one better than thee in the world, and after thee I shall likewise not create one; thou art my chosen one, and I have made this world apparent on account of thee." *Sad Dar*, chapter 81, p. 56.

[18] *Humans are made of clay and seyyeds of light*
Seyyeds are far removed from the humans' plight.

Go to mourning ceremonies in groups with odd numbers, not even numbers, since it is a bad omen to go in even numbers. In such ceremonies, hookahs should be brought one by one; it is bad omen to bring a pair.

Whoever organizes a mourning ceremony must also be the person to end it. Otherwise, it is a bad omen.

Disinherited by Parents: If parents curse their child, after the child dies, fire flames up from his grave, his sin is inexcusable, and he shall burn in the fire of Hell forever.

Women's blood is ominous.

The blood of seyyeds is ominous (which means they should not be killed).

There is great religious reward for walking to the Shrine of Shah Abdolazim and with three rounds of prayer beads, reciting the salutation to the Prophet Mohammad and his family.

If a person born out of wedlock goes on pilgrimage to the Shrine of Bibi Shahrbanu, he or she will have a nosebleed, and if a religiously unclean man, a rogue, looks at its *qanat*, its water will lessen.

"No snow accumulates but rather melts on any land in which there is a treasure or someone buried; and one of the signs of a buried person is that the land is in ruins and uncultivated; and if basil has grown on it, they must know that someone is buried there; and if they see sesame plant or eggplant on the slope of a mountain away from an inhabited place, they should know that someone is buried there; and if the land is salty and has as much as a cowhide of good land on which there is a pleasing flower, they should know that someone is buried there who is deserving of love; and if they see a large number of wolves but no carrion, they should know that someone is buried there; and if they see a large number of vultures but no carrion, they should know that someone is buried there; and when it rains and water gathers on a part of the land without the existence of a pothole, they should know that someone is buried there...; and when they see a pheasant and a francolin both landing there and happily playing, or see honeybees gathering unexpectedly somewhere, or see a tree one of the braches of which has grown separate from the others in a different direction from all the other branches, they should know that someone is buried there."[19]

[19] *Nowruznameh,* pp. 22-23.

13

Practical Instructions and Rules

If a knife or a jackknife is wielded jokingly at someone, its tip must be struck to ground to prevent bloodshed.

If the names of catastrophic diseases (cholera, plague, etc.) are mentioned, one must bite the space between the thumb and the index finger.

When women are surprised by something, they say, "Face the black mountain."

When drinking water, a man must have his hat on and a woman, her chador. In the absence of a head cover, they must put their hand on their head.

When someone has a wet dream, they say, "Angels removed a curtain before his eyes," or they say, "Earth cursed him."[1]

When with the intention of getting one's wish fulfilled a person steals a tea glass during a religious mourning ceremony, once the wish is fulfilled, he must buy six tea glasses and take them to the place where the ceremony was held.

If a person with the evil eye praises someone, in order to protect him from harm, using a knife, a line must be drawn across his footprints, or a piece of the pant string or clothing of

---

[1] This is similar to Zoroastrian thinking on the subject, since in the Avesta it is stated that a man's sperm should not be wasted and must become a child. When it is wasted, it is a cardinal sin. See: The Vendidad, Sections 74-76 and 102-107.

"(2) Piety is not to harm one's own seed and semen and not to give it to undeserving people. (3) When he does not hold his own sperm in respect, Paradise in the heavens shall punish him and before Ohrmazd, reveal his animosity and not allow his soul to enter Paradise." *Bundehesh*, p 146.

the person with the evil eye must be burned and the ashes rubbed on the nose of the victim.

When someone is praised, in order to prevent him from becoming a victim of the evil eye, they must immediately touch the dust on the sole of the shoe of the one who has given praise and rub the dust on the navel of the one being praised.

People should blow into their own sleeve when running or in order to carry out a task quickly.

In order to get rid of a guest, a sleeping cap is placed on the top of a ewer under a downpipe facing the same direction as the Qibla, or a pestle is placed vertically in a firepit stove, or salt is sprinkled in the shoes of the guest.

Children believe that if they place a peacock feather between the pages of a book or a copy of the Koran and sprinkle it with a little powdered sugar, the feather will procreate its own children and multiply.[2]

One should pull down the wick of a lamp and let it go out by itself. Puffing at it shortens life.[3]

For excessive laughing, they look at their thumb or the space between their thumb and forefinger and say, "Oh God! Do not be angry with me."

A person who sews his or her own clothes must keep a piece of their own clothes between their teeth for the entire time that it takes to sew.[4]

When people come out of the public bathhouse, they say, "May the warm water keep you well." The response is, "Good health to you as well."

If you are attacked by a wolf at night, strike a match. The flame of it melts the fat of the wolf's eyes. And if you are attacked by a dog, just lie down.

---

[2] *Between the pages of a Koran, I saw a peacock feather laying*
I said: I think your status is beneath the place where you are staying
It said: Hush, I say, everyone with some beauty will at last,
No matter where he steps, be allowed to pass
        Sa'di

[3] This is reminiscent of blocking the mouth in a fire temple. It is done in order not to pollute the fire.

[4] Because a dead person cannot hold anything between his teeth.

It is obligatory to make a sacrifice when digging the foundation of a house, a bathhouse, or a reflecting pool to prevent bloodshed.

When the house door is being installed, a butcher must put his hand in the sacrificial blood and smear the door.[5]

When women hear something they have not heard before, they place one leg of their *chaqchur* pants [footed trousers] on their heads.

When there is a conversation about a bad thing, such as death, illness, or harmful animals, people say, "The hour is heavy."

If someone breaks a lot of dishes and other things, in order to get himself free of such a habit, he must steal food, then go and eat it by a body of water.

When people buy a new house, they must first send a mirror and a copy of the Koran there and express congratulations and good wishes and curse Satan, who is the enemy of happiness and tranquility.

When someone makes a wish and asks something of three people riding the same horse, whatever the response, they must do as told.

When people drink water at sunset, they must toss a little of it behind them and say, "The dead are thirsty."

In order to make a letter reach its destination quickly, they write 2468 (2=b, 4=d, 6=u, 8=h) for *Boduh*, which is the name of an angel who delivers letters.[6]

If someone's name is mentioned and that person enters the room, he or she is undoubtedly a religiously legitimate child.

A person who wants to get up early in the morning says to his or her pillow, "May you be blamed for the sins of the miller, the customs agent, and the undertaker if you wake me up late."[7]

To eliminate the ominousness of the number 13, when counting, instead of saying thirteen, they say "add one."

---

[5] Such bloody sacrifices are specific to Semite Arab and Jewish tribes. It is particularly common among the Jews.

[6] In his *Seh Maktub*, Mirza Aqa Khan Kermani had mistakenly thought that *Boduh* was taken from the Persian word *"bodo"* [run].

[7] This is a sort of autosuggestion.

In order for the wound of an Aleppo boil to heal in less than one year, instead of calling it *salak* [Aleppo boil] call it *mahak* [little moon].

When the noon cannon is fired, one must kiss the tip of the finger and touch the forehead with it.

When returning from a funeral service, before entering the house, it is necessary to put your shoes on the wrong feet.

If a woman's chador gets a burn during a funeral ceremony, she must pawn her chador, buy as much dates as the weight of her chador, give them away as charity, and then take back her chador. If she does not, her husband will die.

Whoever pulls out his 120-year-old tooth must not show it to anyone. If he does, he will die and the person who has seen it will live for 120 years.

If one hears a noise in the ear, it is an indication that someone has remembered him. He must then try to remember each and every one of his or her friends and acquaintances. When the noise in the ear stops upon remembering one of them, that is the person who had remembered him.

If while walking on the road a person's foot hits the back of the foot of another, the two should turn toward each other and lock their little fingers together, otherwise, they will have a fight.

One should not circumambulate another person, because he or she will become the diverter of calamity for that person. If anyone does so, to ward off the evil consequences, he or she must go backwards the same way.

When they count the strands of a woman's hair, they must say, "One date, two dates...," otherwise, she will be the victim of the evil eye and her hair will fall out.

When something is lost, a person should make a knot in some corner of their clothes and say, "I block the luck of the daughter of the King of Fairies." Or they should say, "Satan, give me what is mine and I will give you what is yours."

When a thin string or a silk thread is tangled and knotted, if someone wants to unravel it easily, they should say, "Unravel or I will give you to a Jew."

If an unpleasant event happens to someone but he or she gets through it happily, it is evident that he or she had a copy of the Koran at hand. To rid oneself of the evil consequences, one must put some money under one's head at night and in the morning give it to a beggar.

When lighting a lamp, special prayers are recited and the people look at greens, or a mirror, or a horse, or a beautiful face.[8]

If a woman gets into the habit of eating one bite of bread and goat cheese after her meal, she will never have a co-wife.

Bread is God's bounty. If it falls on the ground, it must be picked up, kissed, and placed in the hole of an outer wall. Otherwise, famine will ensue.

If something gets lost, the woman should recite the "Al-Hamd" verse from the Koran and make a knot in the corner of her chador, and when it is found, she should recite the "Qol ho-Allah" verse and open the knot.

When cutting cloth for new clothes or when a happy event occurs, people say, "May Satan go blind; may Satan go deaf."

If a woman is in her menstrual period and touches certain flowers, they will wilt.

If there is a conversation about someone being beautiful, in order to prevent her from becoming a victim of the evil eye, those talking must look at the tips of their noses and touch them with their fingers.

When someone sees a beautiful person or a pretty animal or anything pretty, they must say "Masha Allah"; otherwise, they could become the victim of the evil eye and suffer some calamity.[9]

If people step over someone who is sleeping, they must mention his name.

To ward off diseases and disasters, such as earthquakes, plague, and pestilence, and even to ward off enemies and a solar or lunar eclipse, people need to engage in congregational prayers and *Ayat* prayers, because such disasters are the result of sinning.

---

[8] This custom was also common during the Sassanid period. *Denkard*, 8, 20, 44.

[9] "(1) When one sees anything that is welcome to the eyes, it is requisite to say 'in the name of the Creator.' (2) Let it be known, because if they do not say 'in the name of the Creator' and an injury happens to that thing, or a disaster occurs, one becomes a sinner." *Sad Dar*, chapter 15, p. 14.

When children wish for two people to have a quarrel, they hit the thumbnail of one thumb with the thumbnail of the other.

When people want a traveler not to return, they hit the ground with a "used earthen cooking pot" or a black stone.

14

Some Idioms and Proverbs

Idioms, proverbs, and lexical allusions have a special connection with common people's mentality. It seems that in order to express what they see and their emotions, common people do not need to know the derivation of words and the logical research regarding their meanings. They express what they feel as a result of their observation with the first simile that comes to mind. The closer that these words are to the mentality of common people, the stronger and livelier they are; and the creation of language appears to be directly related to such words and idioms. Among them are words that have been created by imitating the sounds of animals and objects,[1] as are the first words of children, which are also similar imitations, such as: *bahbahi* [yummy], *pufeh* [a baby's word for anything warm to eat or to drink], *juju* [a baby's word for bugs], and so on. And then such words have acquired their own meaning in the language, such as: *atseh* [sneeze], *ghogha* [uproar], *kuku* [cuckoo], *qahqaheh* [guffaw], *verzadan* [blabber], *hort keshidan* [slurp], *veng* [whining], *pif* [pyoo], *tof* [spit], *miyo-miyo* [meow, meow], *khor-khor* [snore], *hen-hen* [huh], *vaq-vaq* [woof, woof], *ghar-ghar* [caw, caw], *jik-jik* [chirp, chirp], *chahchaheh* [trill], *ar-ar* [hee-haw], *dang-dang* [ding-dong], *bam-bam* [boom, boom], *ghol-ghol* [gurgle], *chek-chek* [drip, drip], *qerch-qerch* [crunch, crunch], *vez-vez* [buzz, buzz], *chelep-chelep* [splash, splash], *shelep-shelep* [splash, splash], *sherep-sherep* [splash, splash], *keh-keh* [icky, poopy], *malach-malach* [munch, munch], *haf-haf* [woof, woof], *lef-lef* [gobble, gobble], *gor-gor* [snap, crackle, pop], *tap-tap* [lub-dub], *jelez-o velez* [fizz], *noch-noch* [tch tch], *pech-pech* [whisper],

---

[1] Onomatopoeia.

sher-sher [whoosh, whoosh], *koruch-koruch* [crunch, crunch], *daq-daq* [knock, knock], *khesh-o fesh* [froufrou], and so on.

There are also idioms and allusions that have assumed a figurative image in language and are used metaphorically. For example, the names of various parts of earthen jugs are taken from human body parts: *dahaneh* [mouth, opening], *labeh* [lip, edge], *gardaneh* [neck], *dasteh* [hand, handle], *shekam-e kuzeh* [belly of the jug], *kamar-e kuzeh* [waist of the jug], *payeh* or *tah-e kizeh* [foot or bottom of jug].[2] There are also idioms such as: *ab-e zir-e kah* [water under the straw], which is used to describe a sneaky hypocrite; *damaghash chaq ast* [his nose is fat] and *nanash tu-ye rowghan ast* [his bread is in ghee] for a wealthy person; *dastash beh dahanash miresad* [his hand can reach his mouth] for a middle-class person; and *dastash kaj ast* [his hand is crooked] for a petty thief.

There are many such idioms that are beyond the scope of the present book. Here, I will only mention the idioms that are related to the beliefs of the common people:

Hello is health.

Hello is recommended; responding to it is a religious obligation.

I swear on the blade of the sun.

I swear on light of the lamp.[3]

---

[2] It is because of the similarity of the parts of the human body and those of the earthen jug that, in his materialistic philosophy, the poet Khayyam continuously seeks the particles of the human body in the jug of wine, speaks to the earthen jugs in the potter's workshop, and remembers their past life on earth:

The jug was once like me, a brokenhearted lover
Bound by the curls of the tresses of a beloved
The handle you see upon its neck
Is a hand which was once 'round the neck of a beloved

[3] Respect for light and greeting lamps are among pre-Islamic customs in Iran. Ferdowsi says:

[I swear] on the shining star, the dark earth
On bright souls and pure hearts filled with mirth
That all of our hearts are full of love for you
We all desire to see that face that is you

From *Vis and Ramin*:

Now shall I light a fire that is good

I swear on the light of the Great Stone.
I swear on the stove [virility] of your father.
I swear on *Shah-e Cheragh.*
Charity diverts calamity.
Guests are friends of God.
Business people are friends of God.
Hearts communicate.
"When" is the work of the devil.
Go change your forehead.[4]
May all his time buried in the earth be the length of your life [said as a condolence]. Or: So-and-so gave his life to you [said when reporting someone's death].
One glance is religiously allowed (regarding a girl or a woman a man wants to marry, or wants to see to possibly marry).
Fire breeds ashes (reverse heredity influence).
Going on pilgrimage lightens one's bones from sin.
I hope the earth does not report to him (when they speak ill about a dead person).
The dead are free on Friday eves.
One rib of the people from Isfahan is religiously unclean.
He has woken up on his left rib [wrong side of the bed].
Wednesday eve belongs to Aisha.
His left eye fell on [developed enmity toward] so-and-so.
Apples fill you up.[5]
May the pain and calamities of someone strike the life of someone else. [The first person is nice, kind, or talented and the second one is the opposite.]
May his hand be under the head of so-and-so. [Wishing so-and-so to suffer what the first one has suffered.]
Hitting his crow with a stick [spying on someone].
Leeks take after their seeds, and Hasani after his dad. [The apple doesn't fall far from the tree.]

With heaps of musk and aloeswood
Before the devout of the earth right here
Upon that fire make your oath sincere

[4] According to Islam, the future of everyone is predestined and written on his forehead. The idiom here allusively means: Misfortune has no remedy. (See the story of "Mah-Pishani.")

[5] *Pomegranates are dastardly and apples leave you filled inside*
Thus bestow me a quince, be you a man who is bona fide.

They say the following when they see a lit lamp: "Greetings to you, *Shah-e Cheragh*."

When you mention a dog's name, get hold of a stick. [Said jokingly when a person arrives after his name is mentioned, akin to "speaking of the devil."]

They lit his hair on fire.[6]

One hair of this person's body is not on the body of that person. [The second person does not have the good qualities of the first person.]

There is no two that does not become three.[7]

A son lights the stove of the man.

An open mouth will not be without its daily bread.

Preparing a Last Will and Testament is a blessing (prolongs life).

My eyes at the soles of your feet (to prevent the evil eye).

Seven copies of the Koran in between [to protect you from a bad incident].

Two hundred bouts of crying await every laughter.

My thumb got the news. ["It dawned on me" or "I got a whiff of it."]

My heart skipped a beat.

The relationship between what is religiously permissible and your spouse should not be disrupted.[8]

The marriage of a male and female cousin is made in the empyrean.

Water you have not asked for is a fulfilled wish.

The door of his house is closed (he has no comings and goings and has no son after he dies).

The key to the door of his house fell on the roof (he had no heirs, and his home was taken away).

---

[6] This is a reference to the story of "Simorgh and the Dragon" and the story of Zal [in the *Shahnameh*], who was raised by Simorgh, and when his father takes him back from Simorgh, Simorgh gives Zal one of its feathers to burn when in need, in order to have Simorgh come to his rescue.

[7] *O Light of Truth, 'tis my petition*
Write this third book, as three is tradition
          Rumi

[8] Angels are disgusted by the smell of the one who initiates a divorce.

May his ear ring (when speaking of someone who is absent).

No one sleeps in his house on the night he dies.

Placing a horseshoe in fire [being anxious for a traveler to return].

Its talisman was brought by a Jew.

He smells like halva (he has gotten old and decrepit).

Its soil shackles you. [Said of a city or country that you visit and do not want to leave.]

Our hats squished together [we got into an argument].

Putting your foot in someone's shoe [sticking your nose in someone else's business].

The meaning is sitting behind the door.

Far from now (this is said when conversation is about the relationship of a dead person and someone who is still alive).

Have you eaten a sparrow's head?[9]

"Gem belly" is an expression that refers to a woman who has a son.

They have sprinkled the dust of the dead around him.

A person drinks the water of his or her own heart.

He has no star in the seven heavens.

---

[9] Since sparrows chirp and make a lot of noise, this idiom is used for a garrulous person.

15

Things and Their Benefits

Turquoise brings good luck, and putting a turquoise ring on your finger facilitates your affairs.[1]
Snakestones bring about good luck.[2]

Nazar Qorbani (sheep's eye, which on the day of the feast of sheep-killing, when the sheep is killed and its eyes are dehydrated) is effective for warding off the effects of the evil eye (especially if it is stolen). They tie it together with a piece of rock salt and green glass donkey beads on a string and hang it on the particular child's hat or on the top of his or her shoulder.

Bebin-o bettarak [see and burst], *koji-ye abi* [blue beads], *haft mohreh* [seven beads], tiger tooth, deer hoof, wolf nail, *cheshm-e baba quri* [large glass bead that resembles a blind eye], and blue cloth are good for warding off the effects of the evil eye.

When a stone is left in the sun for a long time, it will become a ruby:

They say that stone turns to ruby with patience
Yes it does, but not without blood and toil

They say that if a virgin girl pounds lye with vinegar under a downpipe facing the same direction as the Qibla, it is good for neutralizing spells and black magic.

If a person carries hazelnuts (or almonds or walnuts) used in *samanu*, he will be immune to all calamities.[3]

Wolf fat brings disaffection.

---

[1] "They say looking at it brightens the eyes." *Borhan-e Qate'*. "Because of its name and because of its preciousness and the sweetness of seeing it, and its benefit is that it prevents the effects of the evil eye and being harmed in sleep." *Nowruznameh*, p. 28.
[2] The way to acquire them was mentioned earlier.
[3] *Kolsum Naneh.*

Eating fish and yogurt together is bad.[4]

The urine of a preadolescent boy renders black magic ineffective.

Urine helps heal wounds.

Urinating behind a wall causes adversity.

Urinating in the hot water pool of a public bathhouse causes forgetfulness.

Urinating in a public bathhouse causes blindness.

To counter spells, urinating on the big toe in the public bathhouse is recommended.

If a frog urinates on someone, he will develop a fever.

A person who burns onion skins and eggshells together will be haunted by the jinn.

When someone is afraid, they put salt in his mouth.

Carrying camel hair helps ameliorate intermittent fever.

To make a guest leave, they pour salt in his shoes.

Salt is praised and respected by common people, and eating someone else's bread and salt makes a person indebted.[5] A person who acts in the contrary is called *namakbeharam* [religiously violating respect for salt, i.e., ungrateful] and *namaknashnas* [not acknowledging hospitality, i.e., rude].

A salt-less hand is a hand that does not do good deeds and is without blessing. In idioms, whatever lacks salt is tasteless and insipid, such as a dull face. Also, very religious people swear and curse on salt. For example, they say: "May my salt grab you or strike you."[6]

It is said that the ancient Iranian king, Kayumars, discovered salt when, in the dessert, they brought the cooked meat of the hunted animal on a slab of stone. When he tasted it, he found it to be more tasty than usual, and he found out that the stone on

---

[4] Saying: "Said the Angel of Death: Yogurt and fish? Is that your wish?"

[5] Idiom: "He ate his salt and broke his saltshaker."

[6] *First, noble Ramin took an oath*
   On God, the Lord of the Universe
On the shining moon and bright sun
   On auspicious Jupiter and pure Venus
On bread and salt and the religion of the Creator
   On bright fire and the eloquent soul
   From *Vis and Ramin*

which the meat had been served was rock salt. The use of salt in food then became common. They surmised that God had provided for that event so that His creatures would learn to use salt. In *Abjad* calculations, the Persian word for salt, *namak*, and Ali each amounts to 110, and it is possible that salt is held as sacred for this reason.

Making vinegar could have consequences of good or bad omen.[7]

If Nisan rain [akin to "April showers"], which occurs seventy days after Persian New Year, Nowruz, falls on the hair of anyone, it increases the amount of hair, and if given to an ill person, he recovers.

If a person eats the tumors in meat, he will develop tumors.

Yogurt and lettuce prolong life.

The tobacco residues in a clay pipe can kill snakes.

Saliva is good for wounds.[8]

The smoke from the burning of the droppings of a jenny is beneficial for all swellings and diseases.

Cobwebs are beneficial for broken bones and cuts, and for stopping bleeding.[9]

It is religiously rewarding to eat *torbat-e Seyyed al-Shohada* [a bit of the soil of the tomb of the Sire of Martyrs (Imam Hoseyn)] at the beginning of every month.

Eat yogurt and place the bowl under your head to go to sleep.[10]

Any girl who eats sweets that are tossed over the head of a bride will find a good husband.

---

[7] On the whole, good and bad omen cover an extensive arena. From planting to keeping animals to people and anything they do could be good omen for one person and bad omen for another, and all this becomes clear after testing it.

[8] "If saliva from the human mouth is rubbed on injuries, it is beneficial, and it also benefits humans with insect and reptile bites and is the antidote for all bites, especially if the person is hungry or thirsty, and the saliva of a person who is hungry kills all creatures." *Hezar Asrar*.
Saliva is also used in sorcery and for warding off the evil eye, etc.

[9] "Place cobwebs on the area that is bleeding, and it will stop bleeding." *Nozhat al-Qolub*.

[10] Because yogurt makes a person sleepy.

A person who has a sore throat should make his throat religiously unclean [drink alcohol] to recover.

In order to prevent damage to an automobile, they hang *nazar orbani* and *koji-ye abi* [blue beads] in front of it [on the rearview mirror].

To create affection, they place a horseshoe in fire.

Burning frankincense and wild rue every morning facilitates affairs.

Making vinegar and raisins causes homelessness and exile.

Feeding a baby mare's milk will ensure that he never gets the whooping cough.

If someone is frightened, someone dips a diamond or the latch of a door in water three times and makes that person drink the water.

When the corner of the lip has a wound or a fever blister, it is the sign of Satan having put a harness on it. It should be hit with a door latch to get well.

If people do not want to see someone again, they crush a used earthen cooking pot on the ground behind him.

The life of anyone who sees a 120-year-old tooth gets prolonged.

If vinegar turns in the vat (becomes wine or becomes tasteless), someone in the household will die.

Chewing gum causes one to have a sparse beard, and if the gum is swallowed, it causes urinary retention.

If bitten by a rabid dog, some of its hair is burned and put on the wound.

Castor beans prevent the effects of the evil eye.

Swallowing fingernails or toenails causes hunger disease.

Swallowing cat's hair causes hypochondria.

Cheese decreases intelligence.[11]

Eating the inside fiber of a reed pen, if it has not seen the sky, increases intelligence.

Turnips increase common sense.

Cow gallstone is good for fattening. On a moonlit night, a person should disrobe on the roof and rub it over their entire body, except for the nose, since it will also make the nose fat.

---

[11] Donkey cheese as well as donkey meat are disapproved by religious law.

If someone is fed collyrium, he will lose his voice.

Any woman who swallows the foreskin of a boy after he is circumcised will deliver a boy.

Noisy pinwheels and other toys cause illness.

Taking the nuts in uneaten *samanu* and using them as capital for starting a business will make the person rich forever.

Anyone who drinks the water of Chaleh Square in Tehran will develop Aleppo boil.

All foods and medicines are either "cold" or "warm," and the constitution of individuals, according to the medical knowledge of the common people, is of four kinds: hot temperament, moist temperament, dry temperament, and cold temperament. To moderate their physical constitution, they must eat foods that are opposite to their own physical constitution and temperament, and whenever the effects of any of the temperaments becomes dominant, they should eat food from the opposite temperament to achieve moderation.

Good and bad human milk transmits its effects to the temperament, character, and habits of the child. For example, when people curse someone, they say such things as "I spit on the milk you nursed" and "May the breast that nursed you burn," and when they wish to praise someone, they say, "Bravo to the mother's milk that he had."[12]

Turtle eggs and the brain of newborn puppies are used in sorcery.

Black velvet that has not been washed is good for whooping cough.

Rabbit blood is good for tuberculosis.

If they put makeup on the part of raw meat that looks like a doll and wrap it in a cloth and bury it in a house, there will be quarrelling in that house.

Black magic does not work on a person who eats pork.

"And among the attributes of gold is that, first, seeing it brightens the eyes and brings joy to the heart; second, it makes a man brave and increases knowledge; third, it enhances beauty,

---

[12] It is believed that Genghis Khan was nursed on wolves' milk, and for this reason, he became bloodthirsty.

refreshes youth, and delays old age; and fourth, it heightens pleasure and is endearing in the eyes of people."[13]

"If they apply collyrium to the eyes with a gold applicator, it makes the person immune to night blindness and watery eyes and enhances vision; and if they place gold anklets on ankles, they hunt more bravely and happily; and any injury caused by gold heals faster... and drinking water from a golden jug immunizes the person from dropsy and brings happiness to the heart."[14]

"And if someone buries gold in the basement without placing it in an earthen pot or a copper or glass container and after a year goes back to it and does not find it and thinks that someone has stolen it, it is not stolen; it has sunken into the ground, since pure gold sinks further down every day to reach water."[15]

"Ruby is a gem that is a fragment of the sun and is the king of the non-melting gems, and its advantage is that it has rays and fire does not affect it, and it can cut all stones, with the exception of the diamond, and its benefit is that it prevents cholera and the detriments of thirst."[16]

Egg yolk is good for virility and for strengthening the chin.[17]

Dropping eggshells on streets will cause fighting and quarrels.

The skin of dragons can only burn with a fire of onion and garlic skins.

[13] *Nowruznameh*, pp. 20-21.

[14] Khayyam, *Nowruznameh*, pp. 21.

[15] *Nowruznameh*, p. 23.

[16] *Nowruznameh*, p. 27.

[17] Idiom: "He has applied egg yolk to his chin."

Plants and Seeds

*K*harbozeh melon and honey are incompatible foods to
eat together.
Pickled walnuts could have good or bad omen effects.

Chewing dry rice causes sparse beard.

Placing rice under the bedding makes it religiously unclean.

Feeding a cat catnip makes it drunk.

The seeds of muskmelon cause homelessness and exile.

Consuming chickpeas soaked overnight for forty mornings
opens your larynx.

Spreading the seeds of broomcorn in the room results in a
quarrel.

Any person who eats the cap of a date will get pimples on
his face.

Applying woad to eyebrows strengthens the person.

Henna cures split hair.

When people eat *kharbozeh* melon, they should look at
themselves in the mirror to see how fat they have become, and if
they look at the backs of their hands, they will become fat and
white, like *kharbozeh* melon.

Spreading nigella seeds in the room results in a quarrel.

Planting eggplants, potatoes, clover, and barley can result in
good or bad luck.

Oleander bushes can be good or bad omens.

Pistachio and walnut trees can be good or bad omens.

If you plant zucchini, when it starts creeping, you will become a homeless exile.

Every grain of rice is inscribed with the Koranic verse, "*Qol
ho Allah*." One should not step on them.

A person who sleeps under a walnut tree will become
haunted by the jinn.

If you bite watermelon rind you will become bald.

Cracking and eating roasted watermelon seeds after eating watermelon eliminates the benefits of the watermelon.

The first fruit created by God was watermelon. After mastering its creation, He collected the seeds of other fruits and either placed them in the middle of the fruits, or made eating them easier.[1]

One person alone should eat the two ends of a *kharbozeh* melon. If two people eat it, they will start a fight.

The Mohammedan flower [rose] grew from a drop of sweat of Mohammad on the ground.[2]

---

[1] This issue verifies Darwin's theory regarding the philosophy of evolution.

[2] Verses from a popular song from Kerman:

> *On Saturday near the bridge along my course*
> *I saw the footprints of Ali and the hoof prints of his horse*
> *From the pure chest of Mohammad, sweat arose*
> *And dripped to the ground, giving rise to a rose*

According to an old legend, the red rose, which is called *khun-e Siyavashan* [blood of Siyavash], grew from the blood of Siyavash which dripped on the ground. As Ferdowsi says:

> *The head of that cypress-like figure fell, gored*
> *As into the tub from his body blood poured*
> *Where the tub of blood was ordered to be placed*
> *His armor fell, 'round his body spaced*
> *Right where the toppled tub of blood did flow*
> *Rose a plant from the blood that began to grow*
> *Now, witness the plant that arose due to that slash*
> *The plant that you call Blood of Siyavash*

In a popular song, from the blood of the lip of the beloved grows a cluster of flowers:

> *Last night, my love, as it was raining*
> *Neared the roof's edge, there remaining*
> *I went to kiss her lip, feeling oh so freed*
> *But it was delicate and began to bleed*
> *Its blood dripped into the flowerbed*
> *And a cluster of flowers grew instead*

In popular stories as well as the following song from Jandaq, the reed flute grows from blood:

> *I went to my brother's house with glee*
> *To pick a pomegranate from his tree*
> *My brother came and cut off my head*

When a fruit tree does not bear fruit, two people go to the tree carrying a shovel and an axe. One of them angrily shouts at the tree and says, "We need to cut down this tree; it bears no fruit." And he starts digging the ground by the foot of the tree with the shovel. The other one intercedes. He comes forward and holds the other man's hand and says, "Forgive the tree this time. If it doesn't bear fruit next year, cut it down then." The tree gets scared and bears fruit the following year.

If a pregnant woman eats apples and pears, her baby will become pretty.

Rhubarb grows on the rocks of mountains as a result of thunder and lightning.

Eating large black raisins enhances memory.

One aril of a pomegranate belongs to Paradise. For this reason, when eating a pomegranate, eat all the arils carefully.

If someone offers an apple to someone else, he must press the tip of his finger on it. Not doing so is a sign of disaffection.

Figs, apples, and grapes are fruits from Paradise.

If an onion sprouts in the house, it will result in homelessness and exile.

Raw onions should not be eaten on Fridays.

Mandrake: "It is a plant that resembles humans and grows in China and is upside down, such that its roots are like hair on its head, and the male and female have their arms around each other's necks and have their legs together firmly, and it is said that whoever digs the mandrake out shall die in a few days, and the method for digging it out is that they dig around it so that it can be dug out with little force and then they tie a string on it and tie the other end of the string on the waist of a greyhound and let loose a prey in front of the dog. When the dog begins to chase the prey, the plant is uprooted, and that is why they call it dog-dug, and the dog dies within a few days. It is also called "people's plant," and its male and female can be distinguished, and if they give some of it to a barren woman with cow's milk, of course, she will have a child. If she eats of the male, her child

---

My blood filled a ditch near the flowerbed
The ditch gave the reed...

will be male, and if she eats of the female, her child will be female."[3]

Delphinium is commonly believed to have been cursed and disinherited from its parents. It was a girl, her mother cursed her, and her tongue grows out of the back of her head.

If a person digs out the root of a grapevine, he will die.

Mulberry trees and pine trees should not be cut down, and on the whole, cutting old trees is a sin.[4]

"And it has been said that from eating barley, dirty and corrupt blood that requires vomiting will occur, and also it makes the person immune to blood and bilious diseases, and the physicians of Iraq call it blessed water, and it is a thing that benefits twenty-four types of well-known diseases... And barley oil diminishes bilious symptoms, and wheat diminishes atrabilious symptoms. And they place the husk of barley in a pot and boil it well for someone the nerves and veins of whose legs have become weak and who cannot stand, and place the joints and the knees in the water of barley to recover, and they do the same with wheat... And they say that on the night of a lunar eclipse, if they can, they should plant barley and make bread of the barley to feed the lunatics, which is beneficial, and when the moon shines brightly and is facing Venus, at that time they plant barley, which if fed to any skinny horse will make it become fat, and the goodness or badness of the year appears in barley, such that if barley grows straight and evenly, that year will be a year of plenitude of grains, and if it grows crooked and unevenly, it will be a year of scarcity of grains."[5]

"And water that passes through an unripe wheat or barley farm will reduce exhaustion and eliminate stomach fatigue, and the person shall be immune to thirst and illness until the following year when barley ripens."[6]

---

[3] This segment is quoted from *Jahangiri Dictionary* and *Borhan-e Qate'*. Common people, however, believe that they should carry mandrake with them for good luck.

[4] This idea resembles Zoroastrian thinking that regards planting trees and building as good deeds.

[5] *Nowruznameh,* pp. 30-31.

[6] *Nowruznameh,* p. 32.

Today, as well, it is a common custom among the people in Iran to take as many grains of barley as they have warts on their bodies, recite the "Alam Nashrah" surah and blow with their mouths on each barley grain and touch each to a wart; then they put a spell on all the barley grains and plant them or place them in water, and they believe that by the time the barley grows in the ground or rots in water, their warts will disappear.[7]

---

[7] Marginal notes of *Nowruznameh,* p. 100.

17

Reptiles and Insects

The blood of frogs and lizards is sinister.

The names of harmful insects and animals should not be mentioned at night, since they might show up.

If one kills an animal at night, they must say "Your mate in Baghdad" or say "With its mate," so that its mate does not show up.

Every red bee that is killed brings a reward of one edible date in the next world.

If a person is bitten by a tarantula, that tarantula's mate goes and sits waiting at the top of the house door so that when they are taking the corpse of the bitten person out of the house, the mate can jump on the coffin.

Red bees are infidels, with the exception of the king of the bees, whose name was Ya'sub. He had converted to Islam in the presence of the Commander of the Faithful, Ali. For this reason, they call the Commander of the Faithful the Commander of the Bees and Ya'sub al-Din. The poet Khaqani writes:

At first my soul was an infidel, just like the bees
At last I found my Muslim soul, like the king of the bees

To eradicate bedbugs, if you catch one of them and burn it; the rest of the bedbugs will get scared and flee.

They asked the stink bug where its home was. It said, "A ruined hut in burnt Behnam."[1]

If a human eats lice, he will become an ape.

Do not open your mouth in front of snakes, centipedes, or lizards, because if they count a human's teeth, that person will die.

If you catch a serpent with the left hand, it does not bite.

---

[1] This is the name of a village near Varamin.

Holding a woodlouse in the palm your hand at the Nowruz vernal equinox brings good luck.

Having lice could result in good or bad luck.

A person without lice is not a Muslim.[2]

If people place two dry bricks in a damp place, they will produce scorpions.

If a spider comes in front of a person, he will get rich.

If there is a spider in the room, you should not kill it.

During years with lots of flies and sparrows, there will be no epidemic.

Squishing the scorpion and placing it on the site it has stung will cure the wound.[3]

If one handspan of the head and one handspan of the tail of a snake are cut off and the middle part is cooked and eaten, this will help virility and also make snake poison ineffective for that person.

To ward off snakes, scorpions, and tarantulas, one should recite the following spell out loud:

> *I take refuge in the Lord of Forgetfulness and Oblivion*
> *From the evil of every creature, be it tarantula*
> *or scorpion*
> *Choke them, choke them, O Noah, put a horn,*
> *a horn in them*

And then that person must clap his or her hands loudly, and believe that as far as the sound of clapping can be heard, no snakes or scorpions can pass through.[4]

---

[2] Some people have assumed that the louse is the only creature that is important and is respected in Islam, because on the Feast of Sacrifices in Mecca, any Hajj pilgrim has to sacrifice one sheep for every louse he kills. The philosophy of this ruling, however, is something else. It implies that one should not be dirty in the House of God, otherwise, you will have to pay a penalty, or something like that.

[3] "Whoever is stung by a scorpion, if they kill the scorpion and place it on the spot where it has stung, the pain will be sedated." *Ajayeb al-Makhluqat.*

[4] *I tied the tail of a snake and the stinger of a scorpion*
Together their stinger and tail I pieced
With stings, horned, horned, horn
I greeted the Prophet Noah and was released

One wing of the fly is pain and the other, cure. When it falls into food, it holds the cure wing up. One needs to also sink the cure wing into the food and then eat the food, in order not to be harmed.[5]

The hand of a person who kills a frog becomes "salt-less." In other words, every good deed he does will be unappreciated.

When a snake chases a person, he must cross seven streams of water.

A white snake is the owner of the house, and must not be killed.

Those of the Bakhtiari tribe do not kill snakes. They say that the dervish has not granted them permission.

If you want to drive a bee out of the room, you should say, "Garlic and vinegar."

When cicadas come, the weather gets warm.

If a crab grabs a person, it will not let go until an Egyptian donkey brays or they send a black donkey to the roof and it brays.

If an earwig (a small beetle that lives under the bark of plane trees) goes to the ear of a sleeping person, he becomes deaf.

Tortoise

Ebrahim was invited to dinner by his enemies. They buried a dog under his cooked rice. Ebrahim enters through the door and says, "Shoo!" The dog under the cooked rice comes to life and runs away. Out of embarrassment, the owner of the house goes and hides under a large wooden dough bowl [which, upside down, looks like the shell of a tortoise]. When they go and find him, the wooden dough bowl has stuck to his back.

"(3) Hence it is obligatory to recite the 'Sorush Yasht' prayer to be immune (that) night to all pests, and insects and snakes and scorpions will be unable to harm him. (4) In every house in which they recite the 'Sorush Yasht' prayer, wind shall blow on that house at night, and no harm can come from thieves, evil, and demons. (5) On that day, Sorush will protect that house." *Sad Dar Bundehesh*, p. 131.

[5] Hadith: "If the fly sinks into the food, then they say that one of its wings is poison and the other heals, thus it provides poison and also serves as a cure."

Another version: The tortoise was an old woman. She had a wooden dough bowl on her back in which she had some dough balls. An orphan asked her for some bread. She refused to give it to the orphan, and the dough bowl got stuck to her back.

God wanted to test the patience of His creatures. He killed the mate of the tortoise, and the tortoise cried and cried until it died. God then killed the mate of an old woman. The old woman cried, and then forgot. For this reason, God increased the life of the tortoise to 1,000 years and killed the humans quickly.

18

Birds and Fowls

It is good to have a turtle dove around the house.

Seeing hoopoes and foxes in the morning is a good omen.

Seeing crows and partridges is a bad omen, and seeing two crows is ominous.

Upon seeing an owl, one should say, "Miss Felicity, welcome. We are having a wedding."

The blood of swallows, hoopoes, and greenfinches is sinister.

If an owl cries, it is a good omen, and if it laughs, it is a bad omen.

Keeping hens for eggs could be a harbinger of good or a bad luck. Keeping partridges for eggs results in bad luck.

A hen that lays eggs with double yolks could prove to be a good or a bad omen.

A rooster that sings at the wrong time must be killed or given away; otherwise, its owner will die. According to another version, this act is akin to freeing a slave in order to protect oneself from something bad.

White roosters should not be killed. They are angels.

When an old rooster sings, it says, "What a good year it was, the year before last." Young roosters say, "We didn't see it, we didn't see it."

When a hen shakes its feathers, it will become windy.

When a hen lays sixty-five eggs, it includes a small egg, which should be kept to ensure prosperity.

Keeping a parrot could be a harbinger of good or bad luck.

When a crow caws early in the morning, news arrives from afar or a traveler returns. One should say, "We hope you have good news, a letter coming from our traveler."

When a hen sings on Mondays and Thursdays sounding like a rooster, it is a good omen; but it is a bad omen on other days, and it must be thrown out or given away.[1]

The hands of a hunter who shoots a crow in the morning will become tied, and he will not be able to shoot anything else until that night.

Chicken and sheep should not be slaughtered at sunset, because their sighing causes harm to people.[2]

---

[1] "(1) When a hen utters a cackle in the courtyard of a house, or the rooster crows unseasonably, it is desirable that they not be killed, and it should not be considered a bad omen. (2) Because the reason it is uttering that cackle is that a fiend has found a way into that house, and the hen or the rooster, alone, does not possess the power that would keep the fiend away from that house, and the hen is going to give the rooster assistance by uttering the cackle. (3) Hence, if at any time the chance comes to pass in that manner, it is requisite to bring another rooster, so that they may drive away that fiend through the help of one another. (4) And if a rooster crows unseasonably, it is likewise not desirable to kill it, because the reason may be that which has been stated. (5) For it is declared in religion that there is a fiend whom they call Sej, and in every house where an infant lives, that fiend strives to cause some misfortune to come upon that house. (6) So it is necessary to keep a hen and a rooster on watch, so that they may smite that fiend and force it to the road away from that house." *Sad Dar*, chapter 32.

"In remedying the sound of animals that occasionally sing with laughter, and also the singing of ill-omen people, which is sinister and inauspicious, in *Baznameh* [Book of Falcons] of Kasra Nushirvan, it is stated that when an animal makes a great deal of noise, after the passage of fifteen days from the beginning of the month, during the second fifteen days, one should feed it greens from gardens and everything that grows on farms, and it should be kept hungry until noon and then fed until full. It will reduce the noise." *Qavanin al-Sayyad*, chapter 30.

No prosperity remains in a house
In which a hen sings like a rooster
            Sa'di

[2] "They must absolutely avoid the killing of sheep with cruelty, since in *Astut Kar* it is stated that the punishment for those who kill sheep with cruelty is that the hair of those sheep become as sharp as blades and will kill the person who has killed them with cruelty." *Shayest Nashayest*, 8, p. 128, published by Navadia.

"(1) It is greatly vital to refrain from much slaughter of animals and cattle. (2) Because it says in revelation that, for everyone who slaugh-

Pigeons do not lay eggs in the lunar months of Ramazan and Moharram and do not have chicks.

The nightingale has seven babies every year, of which one becomes a nightingale and the rest become garden warblers.

The stork travels to Mecca and back once a year. That is why they call it "Hajji Laklak" [Hajji Stork].

When a hen broods, one of its feathers is passed through its nose.

Falcon: "They have said that it is the king of carnivorous animals, and the king of the herbivorous four-legged animals is the horse, and the king of non-melting gems is the ruby, and the king of melting gems is gold... and the falcon possesses such magnificence that other birds lack... and kings regard seeing it a good omen, and when a falcon lands lightly on the hand without harming and turns toward the king, it is proof that he will acquire a new state."[3]

The nest of greenfinches should not be destroyed.

It is a bad omen when an owl flies by when someone is on the road.

---

ters many animals and cattle, every fiber of the hair of a goat becomes, in that other world, like a sharp sword, and adheres to the soul of that person. (3) And there are several things the slaughter of which is worse and a greater sin, such as the lamb, the kid, the ploughing ox, the war-horse, the swallow bird that catches the locust, and the rooster; and of all of these, the sin is most as regards the rooster. (4) If it becomes a necessity, it is proper to kill a rooster that does not crow, and it is necessary to consecrate its head. (5) Any head of an animal that is not consecrated is not desirable to eat, so that it becomes a righteous gift." *Sad Dar*, chapter 34.

"(1) The protection of sheep and other animals concerns keeping them away from hot and cold weather as well as other blights and keeping them fed with water and plants. (2) Since revelation states that at evening prayers, if the Angel Ashu Firuz comes, he looks at all the four-legged and other animals and birds to make sure they are fed and praises the master and mistress of the house, and if they are hungry, he curses them and goes back. (3) No good deed is better than keeping the four-legged animals and birds in the household fed, especially the young female sheep, and it is improper to kill them unless they are too old and sterile to produce milk." *Bundehesh*, 83, p. 152.

[3] *Nowruznameh*, p. 56.

The sandpiper is a small bird that hunters believe is created as a result of rain.

If a sparrow is poked a great deal or kissed and touched, a cat will catch it.

If a swallow comes to the courtyard of a house and makes a nest, it is a good omen and it should not be harmed.

The crow wanted to learn how to walk like a partridge, but it forgot its own way of walking. That is why it jumps as it walks.

"It is said that the rooster lays only one egg in its lifetime. That is why they call the egg '*beyzat al-foqara*' [the egg of the poor]." A poet has written:

Throughout my life, His Excellency was charitable
Like the rooster's egg, just once, and that is all

And it is said that Satan will not go to "any house that has a white rooster." *Ajayeb al-Makhluqat.*

Birds and fowl are good to have around the house, because when unpleasant events are destined for a member of the household, it will strike the birds instead. They must always be kept well fed.[4]

The bald vulture is a large bird that flies over the houses, and whenever it sees a small child alone, it picks him up and takes him away. If its shadow falls on a person's head, it is auspicious.

Swallows' food is wind.

Anyone who destroys a swallow's nest will die within a year.

Allowing pigeons to make a nest under the roof or the gable roof of the house is a religiously rewarding act.

---

[4] (1) It is stated in revelation that of all the compassion they display in the house, nothing is more obligatory than feeding the cow, bird, or sheep or a four-legged animal they have in the house, and then they can attend to other tasks. (2) Since if night comes and they go to sleep hungry, they curse the master of the house and everyone in that house. (3) And they say, may this master of the house have days when he and his wife and children are continuously hungry, may their bread be insufficient, may these children be annihilated from this house and die, and when they kill something, they must cut off the head of that thing. *Sad Dar*, p. 95.

The hoopoe, or [its other name] *shaneh besar* [a comb on its head], was a newlywed. She was combing her hair in front of a mirror when her father-in-law arrived. She became so embarrassed that she flew away with the comb still on her head.

According to another version, [he was a man who] wanted Belqeys. No matter how he tried, the Prophet Solomon would not allow him to see Belqeys, until finally a demon performed witchcraft for him and he assumed the form of a hoopoe.

It is believed that if one cuts off the head of a hoopoe with a gold coin, it can be used for witchcraft.[5]

Morgh-e Haq [Scops Owl]

He has a quarrel with his sister about inheritance. Because he wanted to take two shares and give his sister one share, the sister breaks off with him and runs away, and he becomes an owl. From that time on, waiting for his sister, he says, "Dear Sis, two shares for you and one for me."

Another version: He had eaten one grain of wheat from the property of a minor, which got stuck in his throat. He keeps saying "haq, haq" so much until three drops of blood drip from his throat.[6]

---

[5] "Catch the hoopoe in the name of Almighty God, His mercy be upon us, and strive to make an austere living condition for it for 24 days, and keep it imprisoned in a cage, and feed it licorice pills, and instead of water make it drink aromatic rosewater, and on day 25, obtain a knife made of red copper and write the Grand Name of God... in talisman script, and this must be at the time when the moon is connected to the horoscope of the person who is the operator... and slaughters it with that knife... and care must be taken not to drip even one drop of its blood on the ground—since the entire operation will be corrupt—then its head must be severed from the body and its heart between its shoulders removed..." Then they make a soup with it and eat it. This is four pages in the book, *Asrar-e Qasemi*, describing the benefits of such filth.
[6] "*Morgh-e shabaviz* [*morgh-e haq*] hangs with its foot from the branch of a tree and says 'haq, haq' until a drop of blood drips from its throat." *Jahangiri Dictionary.*

Sparrow

They say that the chirping of this bird is cursing Fatemeh Zahra. Hence, it is a good deed to torment the sparrow, destroy its nest, and grab its chicks and give them to children.[7]

According to another version, the sparrow is an infidel, because at night it sleeps on its back and is afraid that the sky will collapse on it.

Some people religiously forbid using a knife on hens and keep the hen with the intention of not killing it. Then, any calamity that might target a member of the household will strike that hen instead.

If you grab a dying sparrow under its tail, its life cannot leave its body.

When roosters and pigeons sing in the morning, they are chanting fervent prayers to God.

Homay is the name of a famous bird known for eating bones. Sa'di says:

The legendary bird Homay has the noblest of features
For it eats bones and does not harm any creatures[8]

"And one group has said that it is the vulture that eats carrion and there is an abundance of its kind, and Homay is known for being auspicious, such that they say that if its shadow falls on any person, that person shall become a king and achieve prosperity, and its name is the stem of the word Homayun, which means fortunate... It has been seen in a book of history that on islands near China and Arakan, strange birds come together... and they have written in this book that Homa is a bird that is as large as a pigeon, its beak is yellow, and its wings are emerald green, and it is a bit white, and its tail is ash-gray, and on that island, it does not land on the ground or the branch of a tree and is always in motion, and is so anxious and in motion that its female lays its

---

[7] It is well known that Allameh Helli, even though he was a qualified religious jurist, before he reached adulthood, would use a ladder to climb the wall and take out the sparrows' chicks.

[8] Of course, the main purpose is: Imagine a bird eating bones. This nearly impossible feat that results in its death is preferable to harming animals.

eggs on the back of the male, and it does not procreate much and does not live more than one year."[9]

Domestic and Wild Animals

Seeing a white horse fulfills one's wishes.

Keeping a zebra is a bad omen.

Seeing a fox early in the morning is auspicious.

Apes are blessedness, and seeing them on the first day of the year is auspicious.

The blood of cats and dogs is sinister.

Having a rabbit in the courtyard of the house could be a good or bad omen.

A dog has seven lives.

A dog howling at night is a bad omen and someone will die. If it howls behind the house door, the people of the house must shudder.

Asb-e chap [off-colored horse] (in other words, a horse which has three white legs and one black leg) is inauspicious.[10]

If a dog looks at a person sitting at dinner and that person does not give anything to the dog, that person will get hunger disease.[11]

---

[9] *Anjomanara Dictionary*:
> *May Homay never cast its noble shadow, tell him so*
> *On that land where the parrot means less than the crow*
>> Hafez
> *Since I see so many of all birds throughout this prison spread*
> *Would it be possible for Homay to cast its shadow on my head?*
>> Mas'ud Sa'd Salman

When thanking each other, common people say, "May God not remove your shadow from our heads."

[10] *Two forelegs and one hind leg all white*
Riding such a horse is not very bright.

[11] Perhaps this idea is a remnant of the respect and attention that ancient Iranians had for dogs, in gratitude for their loyalty and guarding and their need for this animal. Since the conquest of Iran by Islam, however, this animal has been regarded as religiously unclean, but it is unclear whether or not harming it is regarded as a good deed. In *Sad Dar*, chapter 31, p. 25, we read:

"(1) Every time they eat bread, it is necessary to withhold three morsels from their own bodies and to give them to a dog. (2) And it is not desirable to beat a dog. (3) For, of the poor, no one whatsoever is

When eating, if an animal looks at a person's hand, the person must give the animal three bites of what he is eating. Otherwise, he will suffer an incurable illness.

If there is a dog in the house, angels will not go through it.[12]

If afraid of a dog, read the following Koranic verse: "And their dog stretching out its paws on the threshold." This verse is about the dog of "Ashab-e Kahf" [the Companions of the Cave], because at the entrance of the cave, the dog had placed its head on its front paws and was sleeping. For this reason, any dog who hears this verse becomes calm and harmless.

"There is a line in the middle of the nose of a horse similar to the lines on the human palm. It has been said that if the lines are in the form of a fish or a bow, that horse is very auspicious, and wherever that horse is, it will increase the wealth of its owner day by day, and many other horses will gather and add to the blessing of its owner; and if he goes to war, he would of course gain victory over his enemies."[13]

A horse with widespread tail hair indicates that its owner will go to war.

Sur [dun horse]: This refers to a dark gray horse with a black line from its mane to its tail. It is also called "*sul*." Owning such a horse has been considered to be inauspicious, and some say: "Dun horse stirred away from the herd."[14]

"Black horses are auspicious... *Shabdiz* [color of night] is fortunate and blissful. *Korshid* [sun] is slow and auspicious...

---

poorer than a dog, and it is necessary to give a tethered animal bread, because the good deed is great... (6) In the worldly existence, they are the guardians of men and cattle. (7) If there had not been a dog, they would not have been able to keep a single sheep. (8) Every time that it barks, just as its bark goes forth, the demons and fiends run away from the place."

[12] There is a hadith that states, "*lawla anah raht la amir bihadmih*," which means, "If dogs were not one of the species, I would order their total annihilation."

[13] *Farasnameh-ye Hashemi.*

Horses are among the animals that could cast a good or bad omen, and one can make predictions based on certain signs on their bodies, including the colors, curves, and so on. See *Qabusnameh*, *Nowruznameh*, and various *farasnameh*s [books on horses].

[14] *Anjomanara Dictionary.*

And they say that any horse whose color is that of birds, especially white, is better and worthier, and its master at war will always be victorious... A yellow horse with blue or amber-colored eyes that are yellowish, and a horse on whose body there are white or yellow spots, or that is white like a white eagle with red feet, or has less color and a white face, or all forelegs and hind-legs are white, all are auspicious and propitious."[15]

When a cat cleans its forelegs and face in front of the door, a guest will arrive.

When a cat is cleaning its forelegs and face, people say, "If I will get rich, put your foreleg behind your ear." If the cat does that, the person who said it will get rich.

If a cat scratches itself in front of someone, sorrow will come to that person's heart.

When a cat dies, it should be tossed out of the house over a wall.

If a person sprays a cat with water, he will get warts on the back of his hand.

When the lion sneezed, the cat fell out of the lion's nose, which is why the cat is so arrogant.[16]

Black cats are jinn. Anyone who hurts them will become epileptic.

When one feeds a cat, one should say, "In the name of God," so that it can bear witness in the name of God in the next world.[17]

Cats get used to houses and dogs to their owners.

The lion does not bother with a faithful person and does not eat his or her flesh.

The lion is the king of animals.

---

[15] *Nowruznameh*, p. 54.
[16] *In any form, He is the master of the fate of the firmaments*
After all, does the sneeze of the lion not cause the cat
     and its arrogance?
          Khaqani
There is also an idiom: "It is as if you fell out of the lion's nose."
[17] Because while eating, the cat's eye muscles are contracted, common people think that it is ungrateful and closes its eyes intentionally, meaning, "I did not see your generosity."

When the sun is shining while it is raining, it indicates that wolves are giving birth.

Wolves are afraid of naked humans.

The cat was caressed by Morteza Ali on its back. That is why its back never touches the ground.

If a hunter sees a rabbit early in the morning, he will not be able to shoot anything else until that night.

When a rabbit is running, if it is seen from the left, it is a good omen, and if it is seen from the right, it is a bad omen.

If a camel sleeps in front of the door of a house, the owner will die.[18]

A camel's grudge lasts for forty years.

Hyena: "It is commonly believed that to hunt a hyena, people take a tambourine and another instrument near its hole, or hit two stones together, and someone in the tone of a minstrel says, 'Is the hyena at home?' Then another answers, 'The hyena is not at home.' Meanwhile, they slowly widen the hole and tie the hyena's front and hind legs together."[19]

Elephant: Legend has it that the elephant used to be the king of India. His Holiness summoned it. The elephant said, "I have no nose." His Holiness replied, "You will get such a nose that

---

[18]Saying: "This is a camel that sleeps at the door of everyone's house."
[19] Naser Khosrow, says:

Like the hyena that has been intentionally bound
They continue to say that it has not been found

From the margins of *Divan-e Naser Khosrow*, p. 676.
Rumi says:

You grant yourself an excuse in the mire of interpretation
Since, for your heart to not be torn is your only preference.
You tell yourself, I am allowed out of pure necessity,
God will not fault a helpless man due to His benevolence.
But he has faulted you, and like a blind hyena
You do not see the fault due to your own arrogance.
One of the hunters says, the hyena is not inside this place,
Search outside, not in the cave, he continues to state
*   with prevalence.*
He keeps on saying this as he binds it with a rope
And the hyena says, they are not aware of me, engulfed
*   in ignorance*

you won't be able to gather it." And that is how the elephant got its trunk.[20]

The elephant always reminisces about India. That is why they must constantly hit its head with a hammer or an axe.

Louse: If a person's hand is smeared with the blood of a louse and he touches bread dough, he will become an ape. According to one legend, this is how the ape was created.[21]

Baboon: According to another version, one night the infidels who were at war against Ali closed the gate of the fortress on themselves. In the morning, when they awoke, they had all become baboons.

According to yet another version, initially, the baboon used to be a dyer, with his hands always in the vat of dye; that is why his palms are blue. And the baboon was cursed, for he refused a request by one of the imams.

Bear: The bear used to be a bread baker who baked bread, hid it in the kiln, and refused to give it to His Holiness. That is why he was cursed.[22]

Mule: In the Battle of Kheybar, His Holiness Ali was besieged. He yanked off the door of one of the gates of the fortress and stood with his feet on the two sides of the moat. The soldiers would stand on the door, and His Holiness would have them dismount on the other side of the moat. The enemies of His Holiness would load up the four-legged animals with heavy loads to make his blessed hands get tired. All animals refused to step on the door, with the exception of the mule. For this reason, it cannot procreate.

Camel: One of the guests of His Holiness Abraham was offended by him. A message came from God asking him why he offended his guest. His Holiness stood up and went to find the

---

[20] As you can see, this legend was invented due to the two Persian words, *damagh* and *bini*, both of which mean "nose" in colloquial Persian. However, the expression, *Damagh-e shoma chetor ast?* ["How is your nose?"], actually means, "How are you feeling?" Based on this common mistake, this legend was fabricated.

[21] This shows how hated and filthy the louse is. See the chapter on "Reptiles and Insects."

[22] Bears, apes, and black people are from the corrupted human race and are the intermediary between humans and demons, fiends, and fairies. (*Bundahishn*)

guest. He found the guest riding a camel. He placed the guest and the camel on his shoulder. On the way, the camel needed to urinate. At that moment, an angel held the camel's penis facing behind him to prevent His Holiness from being splashed.[23]

---

[23] Proverb: They asked the camel why it urinated backward. It said, "What part of me is like everyone else's?"

19

Some Ancient Festivals
Mehregan

"Next to Nowruz, there is no festival greater than Mehregan. In the same manner that Nowruz is both a public and a private celebration, Mehregan also consists of the observance of a public and a private celebration, and this feast is celebrated for up to six days... On this day, in the past, the kings placed a golden crown with the image of the Grand Luminary on it on their own and on children's heads and rubbed pussy willow oil on their bodies for blessing; and those who on the first day came to the great Persian kings were the Zoroastrian priests, who brought with them seven banquet trays of sugar, citrons, apples, quinces, pomegranates, jujubes, white grapes, and lotus plants, since the pious believe that on this day, all those who eat the abovementioned fruits and rub pussy willow oil on their bodies and sprinkle rosewater on themselves and their friends will be immune to many blights and calamities during that year."[1]

Sadeh Festival

"Sadeh means flaming fire, a fire with high flames, and it is the name of the tenth day of the month of Bahman, on which day Persians celebrate and build many bonfires... and ignite fires on mountains and on plains. The initiator of this festival was Kayumars."[2]

---

[1] *Jahangiri Dictionary.*
[2] *Anjomanara Dictionary.*

Sadehsuzi

This is a festival that is still celebrated by the Zoroastrians of Kerman in commemoration of Jamshid and the customs of ancient Iran. Religious endowments have been allocated for this purpose in Kerman. Fifty days before the Nowruz festival, people gather many loads of brushwood and firewood (*darmaneh*) in Baghcheh-ye Budaghabad [Budaghabad Garden] in the Zoroastrian neighborhood. Adjacent to this garden is a temple-like house, and the Zoroastrian high priest invites the prominent people of the city, and even the foreigners, to that house, in which large amounts of wine, sweets, and fruits are served to them. At sunset, two priests light two tulip-shaped lamps, light the brushwood with them, and sing special songs. When the fire flames up, all the guests—usually several thousand people—circumambulate the fire with cheerful cries and sing the following song:

Thirty days till flowers, one hundred till Sadeh
Fifty days till Nowruz, to that I say, O yea

They drink wine, and the festival ends with cheers. In Kerman, everyone looks forward to the Sadeh Festival, which is of agricultural importance to them, because it is followed by planting seeds and cultivating the land by farmers. These customs are also observed in some of the cities of Khorasan Province.

Dey Bemehr

"The fifteenth day of every Persian solar calendar month is called Dey Bemehr. This day of the month of Dey is that of the feast and festival of the Magi. This day is held most auspiciously, on which they make a face out of flour dough or clay and place it on the road, and render services, as they would to monarchs and kings. Then they burn it in fire. It has been said that this day was the day when Fereydun was weaned and sat on a cow. It has also been said that anyone who in the morning of this day eats an apple and smells a narcissus will spend the entire year in good health and comfort, and that burning lilies on that night ensures safety from famine and poverty for the entire year, and that it is good to donate to charity on this day and to visit the notables and elders. It has also been said that on this day, Zoroaster left Iran. The ancient poet Zaratosht Bahram has composed the following verses:

When the sun bared its face on the mountain that day
On that day that is called Dey-Mehr Day
Zoroaster, the pious, from Iran departed
On his trek, like a cruel cloud weeping, broken-hearted[3]

Kuseh Barneshin [Sparsely-Bearded Man on a Donkey]

"This was the name of a festival among the Parsis. On the first day of the month of Azar, they would put a sparsely-bearded man on a donkey, rub warm salve on his body, feed him warm foods, and have him hold a fan in his hand, fan himself, and complain about the heat. People around him would hit him with snow and ice and offer him something. If someone did not offer him anything, he would splash their clothes with black ink or black mud that he carried with him. He did so up to an allotted time and with the permission of stewards of the city, and if he went beyond that time, he would face reprimand. The Parsis honored this day with respect."[4]

Mardgiran [Capturing Men]

"This is a festival that the Magi observed on the last five days of the month of Esfand. On these five days, women dominate men and take whatever they want from them, and their husbands are dominated by them. On the first day of these five days, people write a *roq'eh-ye kazhdom* [scorpion petition] to get rid of scorpions."[5]

Roq'eh-ye Kazhdom [Scorpion Charm]

The author of *Ajayeb al-Makhluqat* writes that on the first day of the last five days of the month of Esfand, the days of a festival called the Mardgiran Festival, from dawn to dusk, people write three petitions to get rid of insects and reptiles, and they stick them on three walls of the house and leave the fourth wall, which is the front of the house, empty. It is said that on that day, brave Fereydun created a talisman and with it blocked the poisons of insects and animals. And the verification of the fact that he was the writer of the original *roq'eh-ye kazhdom* is that the

---

[3] *Anjomanara Dictionary.*
[4] *Anjomanara Dictionary.*
[5] *Anjomanara Dictionary.*

Parsis write on that petition "in the name of the Creator and in the name of Fereydun," and some Parsis believe that Fereydun is Noah and that is why they clearly write on that petition, "Greetings to Noah in both worlds."[6]

In his *Al-Athar al-Baqiya*, Abu Reyhan Biruni states that to ward off the sting of scorpions, on the day of Esfandarmaz of the month of Esfandarmaz, between sunrise and sunset, common people write the following charm on square pieces of paper: "In the name of God the compassionate and the merciful. In Esfandarmaz month and on Esfandarmaz day, I blocked the left and the right and the top and the bottom to all except for domestic animals, in the name of the Creator and the names of Jamshid and Fereydun, in the name of God, Adam and Eve. God alone is sufficient for me." Then they stick three of them on three walls and stick nothing on the wall that leads outside the room in order for the insects to flee that way. They say that if the talisman is placed on the fourth wall, it becomes ineffective and the insects cannot find a way to escape. They raise their heads toward the window of the house to see that they leave that way.

Pre-Nowruz Festival

A few days before Nowruz, bonfires are lit in the alleyways. Two or three people put on colorful clothes, hang little bells on their tall hats and on their clothes, and put masks on their faces. One of them hits two boards together and sings the following verses:

> *He has come, the fire lighter*
> *He comes one day a year*
> *I am a small fire lighter*
> *I am poor one day a year*
> *Intestines and hollow guts have come*
> *Whatever wasn't there has come*

And the other ones dance and act silly.

At this time, a buffoon with a baboon, a trapeze artist, a roughneck thug, a dancing bear, and other spectacle makers have thriving businesses and sing the following verses:

---

[6] *Jahangiri Dictionary.*

Has Pepper gone and passed?
No, he has not gone, at last
But his eyes have opened even more
Like the testicles of a wild boar
He has eaten bread, but has no gusto
His arms have no bones, as if made of dough
He will not go to the roof today
Save me from ash-e reshteh
My daddy has killed a little goat
My mommy is cooking the potage
My uncle is a spoon maker
My aunt just eats and pees
The girl with one tooth
Is riding a watermelon rind
The watermelon saunters
Right up to the sheriff's house
Dear sheriff, I've got something to say:
I have a heart full of the pain of life
My husband has taken another wife
He has turned his back on me instead
And reduced my amount of daily bread
With this thin flat loaf of bread
How can my son and I be fed?

Chaharshanbeh Suri[7]

This festival occurs on the last Wednesday of the Persian solar calendar. According to Shi'ite preachers, after the events in Karbala, in order to make it easy to distinguish between the Shi'ites and Sunnis, Mokhtar decided that the Shi'ites should make a fire on the roofs of their houses on Wednesday nights, and from then on this became customary. On this day, in order for girls to find good husbands, families make them pass under the Pearl Cannon, then drop small coins in an earthen jug, and at sunset go to the roof and toss it into the alleyway and say, "May my pains and problems go into the earthen jug in the alleyway." Or they fill a jug full of water and toss it from the roof to the alleyway without looking behind them—lest calamity returns—

---

[7] This festival is celebrated more elaborately in Azerbaijan than in other places in Iran. Also see *Tarikh-e Bokhara* by Narshakhi.

and then dump fire on it. On the eve of Chaharshanbeh Suri, girls whose luck in finding a good husband is blocked (meaning, they cannot find a husband) hang a lock tied to a chain around their necks, such that the lock is located on their chests between their breasts; and then at sunset, they go to an intersection. When a seyyed is passing through, they call out to him to come and unlock the lock to have their luck unblocked (and in particular, to find a husband who is a seyyed).

On the same evening, or the eve of the last Wednesday of the Islamic lunar month of Safar, it is believed that if a person makes a wish, places a key with two bittings on the ground, and stands eavesdropping behind the door of a neighbor's room, if the conversation in the room is in accord with what he has wished for, his wish will be fulfilled, and if it is not, the wish will not be fulfilled.

Qashoqzani [Banging a Pot with a Spoon]

If someone in the family is unwell, on the eve of Chaharshanbeh Suri, a member of the family [usually a female] picks up a pot and a spoon, knocks on the doors of neighbors' houses, and without saying anything, bangs the pot with the spoon. The owners of those houses put some food items or money in her pot. If the food is given to the person who is unwell or food is bought with the money and that unwell person eats it, he will recover.

Niyyat [Intended Wish]

On the same evening, people place an earthen jug of water under the downpipe in the direction of the Qibla, and every member of the household makes a wish and drops something in the jug. On Wednesday morning, someone makes a divination with a *Divan* of Hafez, and a preadolescent girl reaches her hand inside the jug and takes out the items one by one and compares each with the result of the divination.

On the eve of Chaharshanbeh Suri, people make three or seven bonfires with dried brushwood or desert thorns, and all the members of the household, young and old, jump over the bonfires and say:

> *Let my yellowness and feebleness be yours*
> *And your redness and cheerfulness be mine*

One must not blow on this fire. Its ashes are later spread at an intersection.

Nowruz

Fifteen days before Nowruz, wheat or lentils are soaked for sprouting, and before that day, spring cleaning is done. And on the eve of the Nowruz celebration, people wear new clothes from head to toe.[8]

On the first evening of the year, there must be lights in all the rooms of the house. The *Haft Sin* spread is prepared a few hours before the winter solstice transition to the Persian New Year.

Haft Sin [Seven S's]

A mirror is placed at the end of the *Haft Sin* spread, and on either side of the mirror, two candelabras are placed, of which as many candles as the number of children in the household are lit. Other items placed consist of: a copy of the Koran, a large loaf of flatbread, a bowl of water with a green leaf floating on the top, a bottle of rosewater, and wheat or lentil sprouts. In addition to sweet mixed nuts, fruits, sweets, and rooster and fish figurines, seven other items the Persian names of which begin with the letter S need to be included: *sepand* [wild rue], *sib* [apple], *siahdaneh* [nigella seeds], *sanjed* [oleaster fruit], *somaq* [sumac], *sir* [garlic], *serkeh* [vinegar], *samanu* [cooked sweet wheat-sprout paste], and *sabzi* [green herbs], in addition to yogurt, milk, goat cheese, and colored hardboiled eggs...

---

[8] Expression: "New clothes after the Nowruz celebration are good for hanging on a minaret" [meaning, everything has its own time and place]. Poor people say:

Nowruz has arrived and we have no new tunic
The old ones are no good, and they make you sick

"Zoroaster said that the spirits of the dead return to their houses during the last five days of the year, and he instructed that people must clean their houses during those days, spread out clean carpets, and set up a spread of tasty and appetizing foods and eat them, in order for the spirits of the dead to gain strength through their scent and energy." Translated from Abu Mansur Tha'alibi's *Gharar-e Akhbar-e Moluk-e Fars*.

At the moment of the transition of the Persian New Year, all members of the household must sit around the *Haft Sin* spread, and they must hold money or a woodlouse in their hand for good luck. If a person is not at the *Haft Sin* spread in his or her own house at the time of the transition of the Persian New Year, he or she will be a homeless exile away from home for an entire year. A person who has a hot temperament should eat yogurt by dipping his finger in it. Those with a cold temperament should eat a little date syrup to balance their constitution. At the time of the transition of the Persian New Year, women should have a pin holding their scarves under their chins; otherwise, their affairs will fall apart.

The signal of the transition of the Persian New Year is when the green leaf floating on the water moves or the egg on the mirror turns. The candles that are burning on the *Haft Sin* with the intended wish of wellbeing must burn all the way down. They must not be blown out, because if they are, that will shorten life. If they urgently need to be extinguished, it must be done with two green leaves.

A woman entering a house on Nowruz morning is a sign of bad omen, and a man entering the house is a sign of good omen. In general, the first person who enters the house must be a person of good omen and, upon entering, must say, "May you have a hundred years like these years." If the owner of the house is a person of good omen, he or she must leave the house and come back. A person who is cheerful and has a good time on this day will be cheerful and have a good time all year.[9]

Prophet Khezr Spread

This spread is similar to the *Haft Sin*, the difference being that this one is prepared on the last Friday eve of the year and lasts until the transition of the Persian New Year. The only additional items are rice pudding cooked in milk without salt, cooked spinach, and *qavut*. The sign that indicates the arrival of the Prophet Khezr is that he puts his finger in the *qavut*.

---

[9] "Anyone who celebrates Nowruz and joins in the jubilations will spend his life in joy and jubilation until the following Nowruz." *Nowruznameh*, p. 5.

Sizdah Bedar [Thirteenth Outside]

This feast is celebrated thirteen days after Nowruz. On this day, all the people must leave the city to go to the countryside to have a good time, entertain themselves, and take strolls, in order to move the bad omen of thirteen to the open fields and deserts. To find a good husband, girls tie blades of grass together and sing:

> *Off with you, number thirteen*
> *When next year comes I'll be seen*
> *Happily in my husband's house*
> *Holding a baby with my spouse*

20

Famous Places and Things

Cypress of Kashmar

It is commonly believed that Zoroaster brought two pine saplings from Paradise and planted them with his own hands, one in Kashmar and the other in Farmad, a village around Tus. As time passed, these two saplings grew tremendously in size and age, and the people believed in their sanctity. It has been said that countless birds had their nests in the branches of the Cypress of Kashmar, and many animals grazed under its shade. When Caliph Mutowakkil al-Abbasi heard about it, he issued an order to Taher ibn Abdollah, who was the governor of Khorasan at the time, to cut down the Cypress of Kashmar, which was in the Nishabur garden, place it on wheeled vehicles, wrap its branches in felt, load them on camels, and deliver them to Baghdad. A number of Zoroastrians who heard about this order promised Taher fifty dinars if he would not cut down the tree, but Taher cut the tree anyway, and according to the author of *Tarikh-e Jahannamay*, by 232 HQ [846-847 AD], that tree was 1450 years old...[1] And when the tree fell, the ground shook in the vicinity and aqueducts and buildings were damaged, and all kinds of birds in countless numbers flew out of the branches of that tree, such that they filled the sky, and the birds with pleasant

---

[1] This calculation seems fairly accurate, because according to the tradition of Zoroastrians, from the advent of Zoroaster to the death of Yazdegerd (in 652 AD) was 1230 solar years (see "The Letter of Tansar," p. 70). Hence, from the advent of Zoroaster to the year of the *Hijra* is 1200 years, when 232 years are added and the seven-year difference between the lunar and solar calendars is subtracted, it is 1425 years, which is only a difference of 25 years from the abovementioned number.

sounds mourned and wailed... And when that tree reached the seat of that Caliph, at nighttime, the Turkish slaves attacked the cursed Mutowakkil and tore his body to pieces.[2]

Siyah Sang [Black Stone]
This is the name of an area in Gorgan, where there is also a spring with the same name. If a group of people with numerous earthen jugs go to that spring, fill the jugs with water, and return and even one of them steps on a worm on the road they are taking back, the water in the jugs of those people will turn bitter. They need to dump it and go back to bring water, while ahead of them one person should go and remove the worms from where they will walk, so that they can pass and go home.[3]

Chah-e Baran [Well of Rain]
On Mount Bundad Hormozd, there is a place in which there is a well. When there is no rain and there is drought for many years, the people of that area grind garlic and toss it into that well, which results in rain, and they have learned that any person who grinds the garlic will die that year.[4]

Ab-e Morghan [Water of the Birds]
This is the name of a spring in the mountainous areas of Semirom and Qomsheh, the water of which is taken everywhere to get rid of locusts. When the water is taken in earthen jugs by someone with the intended wish for any province, birds that are known as starlings fly out of the neck of the water jugs. When the people arrive at their intended destination, they sprinkle the water, which causes a large assembly of starlings that cut the locusts in half with their beaks and kill all of them, making those farms become safe... And, when I was in Fars Province, I myself saw that they had come to Fars Province to get water from Shirvan, and they say that the condition for the water to be effective is not to place the water jugs on the ground but, rather, to hang

---

[2] *Anjomanara Dictionary.*
[3] *Qabusnameh.*
[4] *The History of Tabarestan.*

them on tripods, and when picking them up, not to look at the
neck of the jugs. God only knows.[5]

Gorz-e Rostam [Rostam's Mace]

A popular story is that when Rostam came to Tehran, because he had no money, he had to pawn his mace to buy bread.
In the Chaharsuq-e Bozorg neighborhood, there is a protrusion
on a wall that they call "Rostam's Mace." There is also a popular
idiom: "Here is Tehran, I said, where Rostam's Mace is pawned
for bread."

Rey

The soil of the city of Rey is no good, because the gover-
norship of Rey was given to Ibn Sa'd to have him kill Imam
Hoseyn.

Cheshmeh Ali [Ali's Spring]

Ali had hit the ground with the bottom of his cane near the
shrine of Shah Abdolazim in the city of Rey, and a spring was
created.

Tup-e Morvarid [Pearl Cannon]

There used to be a cannon placed in the Ark Square in front
of the old *Naqqarehkhaneh* that performed miracles, especially
for girls to find a good husband. People would have the girls
pass under it; and common folks believed that the cannon had
come by itself from Bushehr to Tehran.

Rasht

In the city of Rasht, in order for a girl to find a good husband, she is taken to a tannery, where a preadolescent boy unbut-
tons the girl's panties, then they take a little water from the tannery home and pour it over the girl's head.

Monar-e Sar Berenji [Brass Top Minaret]

In Isfahan, for girls to find a good husband, they climb up
the Brass Top Minaret, which is located in the Jubareh neighbor-

---

[5] *Anjomanara Dictionary. Cheshmeh-ye Sar* [Starling Spring] near
Qazvin is also famous for the same reason.

hood. They place walnuts on its stairs, and they sing the following verses:

> *Brass Top Minaret*
> *I must say, don't get upset*
> *My middle needs a grip, all right*
> *A man whose belt is not too tight*

Upon their return home, they crack the walnuts. This ritual is also performed for good luck.[6]

Khatun-e Qiyamat [Matron of Resurrection Day]

In Shiraz, to find a good husband, girls go to the tomb of Khatun-e Qiyamat and circumambulate the stone mortar, which is located in the middle of the building.

Sheykh Baha'i

In Isfahan, there is a public bathhouse the architect of which was Sheykh Baha'i, who designed it in such a way that it is heated with one candle. On Wednesday eve, girls and women go there and pour the water from the bath on their heads with a "forty-key" bowl, girls to find good husbands and women for good luck.

Hammam-e Panjeh Ali [Bathhouse of Ali's Palm]

This bathhouse is in Yazd, and it is believed that Ali's hand had been smeared with henna and when he wanted to go to the bathhouse, he touched the wall adjacent to it. There is now an impression of a palm of a hand on a stone on the wall, and they claim that the bathhouse does not need fuel for heating.

Qabr-e Pir-e Parehduz [Tomb of the Old Cobbler]

This tomb is in Isfahan, and is on a wall. Those who have a wish to be fulfilled take pieces of stone from there and rub them on the tomb. If their stone sticks to the tombstone, their wish will be fulfilled and obstacles in their affairs will be eliminated.

---

[6] Idiom: "She cracks walnuts with her tail." In the Pamonar neighborhood of Tehran, they use the minaret for the same purpose. However, they light candles and recite prayers.

Drinking Fountain

There is a religiously-endowed public drinking fountain on Mount Sahand in Azerbaijan with a gold and a silver cup for drinking water. It is popularly known that if anyone steals them, the cups will return to the fountain.

Little Mount Sorkhab

In Fuman of Gilan, there is a small mountain near the shrine of Imamzadeh Ebrahim. It is reputed that during the time of Caliph Ma'mun, a person by the name of Sorkhab was the governor of Gilan and caused the death of Ebrahim. Through a miracle performed by Imamazadeh Ebrahim, that governor turned into a small stone mountain. Now, people who go on pilgrimage to that shrine, on their way back, throw a rock at that mountain for religious reward.

Sang-e Shir [Stone Lion]

In Hamadan, for a girl to find a good husband, people take oil and pour it on a stone that resembles a lion and has been there since ancient times.

Abu Darda

This is the name of an adobe building and a dome located on the road from Isfahan to the place known as Monarjonban [Shaking Minarets]. Whenever people want to make a wish come true, they go there and cook *ash-e reshteh* or *ash-e barg* and make a figurine out of dough and drop it in the *ash*, or pottage, which they later drop into flowing water. This *ash* is also customarily prepared in the province of Khorasan and the city of Shiraz. The tombs of Baba Qasem and Kaghazgarkhaneh are also used for this purpose.[7]

Gonbad-e Kheshti [Mud-brick Dome]

This is a tomb in the Nughan neighborhood of Mashhad, in which people say someone by the name of Imamzadeh Mohammad is buried, and that it was built during the time of Shah Abbas I. To get their wishes fulfilled, people make a religious

---

[7] There is also a building that is the tomb of Abu Darda in Kashan that is used for the same purpose.

pledge to His Holiness Abbas to give to charity one stone of bread and thirty *sir*s of yogurt, which is distributed among the poor by an old female beggar.

Panjeh-ye Imam [Handprint of the Imam]
In the Chaharbagh neighborhood of Mashhad, there is a rock which people say has the *panjeh* [handprint] of the Imam, and the alleyway where the rock is installed is called Panjeh Alleyway. People light candles there and rub their faces and other parts of their bodies on the rock and beseech the rock for recovery from ailments.

Pir-e Palanduz [Old Saddlemaker]
There is a tomb in Mashhad which was built during the reign of Soltan Mohammad Khodabandeh [reigned 1578-1587 AD]. It is off Safavi Street on Shur Alleyway, and it is very revered by the people of that city.

Shah Gheys
Local people visit this tomb from the first Saturday of the year for up to thirteen Saturdays to get their wishes fulfilled.

Lion Figure
In Fars Province, it is customary to carve a lion body on the gravestone of chivalrous young men, because a lion represents strength and energy.

Mother of Cholera
In the provinces of Kerman and Baluchistan, when there is a cholera epidemic, people cook *ash-e qol hu-Allah* for the Mother of Cholera and make a pledge to a mimosa tree of one stone of castor oil.[8]

Cheshmeh-ye Gheladush
At the height of twenty yards, there are ruins of false arches and a reflecting pool room. It is commonly thought that it had been the castle of Zahhak.

---

[8] Mirza Aqa Khan Kermani.

Niyak

This a place near Asak and a hot spring, which appears as a wall in the mountain surrounded by lattice-work rooms. It is known as the houses of Div-e Sefid [White Demon], who fought Rostam in ancient times. There is a well at its entrance at the side of the mountain.

The Well at Shah Yalmun Shrine

There is a well next to the sepulture of the shrine of Imamzadeh Shah Yalmun in Kashan. To get news from someone who is traveling, women make a wish, go to that well, and look inside. If a coffin appears before their eyes, their traveler has died, and if they see a smiling face, he is alive. The water of that well is also a cure.

Ancient Victory

Four *parasang*s outside of Kashan on Mount Sarak near Jowsheqan, a fig tree has grown on the peak of the mountain which reaches the sky; and hence, it is of interest to the people. It has a special custodian, who every night lights a lamp at the foot of it, and people make religious pledges and pray. It is reputed that when Abu Lo'lo' was fleeing toward Kashan, he arrived at the foot of this mountain and was hungry. Because the infidels had been chasing him and he did not dare to enter the village, he beseeched God, and right then, the tree became full of figs, which he ate to rid himself of hunger and then went to Kashan. People are very enthusiastic about the figs of that tree and believe that it has many benefits. They send its wood along with children, and its fruit is recommended for having children when a woman or a man eats it.

The Well that Leads to Mecca

There is a well in the basement of the Friday Mosque of Kashan that people believe is connected to Mecca, which is merely two days away. For now, however, that well is blocked, and people say that one day a man was passing the well where a woman was washing clothes. The woman became angry because a man who was not of her immediate family had entered without announcing himself, and she ordered the well and the road to Mecca to be blocked. That woman was Her Holiness Fatemeh.

Miracle at the Shrine

In Abbasabad Street of Kashan, which is located in the Posht-e Mashhad neighborhood, there is a place in which a few years ago, two women lost their earrings, and they swore that at that moment they heard a slapping sound and saw that the tongue of one of the women swelled, turned black, came out of her mouth, and she died. Since a miracle had occurred in that place, people bought the place and made it into an Imamzadeh shrine. A picture of His Holiness appeared on one side of the wall, and the face of the woman with the swollen tongue appeared on the other side of the wall.

The Haftvad Legend

There is a castle near the city of Kerman known as the Castle of Seven Daughters. It is said that at the time of Ardeshir Papakan, there was a man who had seven daughters, whose work was spinning wool. One day, one of the daughters went to the city to buy wool. On the way, she saw an apple tree, some of the apples of which had fallen to the ground because of the wind. She picked up one of the apples and put it in her pocket. When she went back home and began to spin the wool, the apple fell into the spinner. From that day on, her productivity increased and improved, and the family's life greatly prospered from selling the wool threads. Then they realized that a worm was continuously growing in the spinner, and that it was because of that worm that they had become so rich. Then they placed the worm in a coffer and took great care of it, to the point that the girl's father, with so much wealth, decided to become a rebel and built a castle, which is still there and is known as the Daughter's Castle. To suppress his rebellion, Ardeshir Papakan started a military expedition toward the Daughter's Castle from Pars, and a severe war ensued. But Ardeshir was defeated in all the battles. The reason for his defeat was that the father of the girl would bring the coffer with the worm to confront the enemy, and because of the worm, he gained victory. Finally, Ardeshir came up with a ruse. He took some wine with him and, dressed as a shepherd, he approached the castle playing a reed flute. He gave wine to the castle guards and asked them about where the coffer with the worm in it was placed. As soon as they got drunk and fell asleep, Ardeshir went to the coffer, killed the worm with his sword, and on the following day conquered the castle. Because of that worm [*kerm*], a city was built in that region, which they called Kerman.[9]

The Plane Tree of the Shrine of Imamzadeh Saleh

It is said that in the old times, there was a small village in Tajrish, where an old woman with many children lived. On the eve of Nowruz, the entire village was decorated with lights and all the children were wearing new clothes and eating tasty foods, except for those in the old woman's house, which was bleak and dismal. One of the children asked the old woman for new clothes. In order not to break the child's heart, the old woman said, "Don't worry, I'll get you new clothes tomorrow." It just so happened that an old man who was their neighbor heard them while he was on the roof. He felt sorry for them, and he brought some sweets and new fabrics and placed them in the entrance hallway of the old woman's house. As soon as the old woman saw them, she prayed and said that she hoped whoever brought them would, God willing, live for a thousand years. On the same day, the old man had planted a plane tree sapling in the courtyard of his own house. Many years passed and that sapling grew, and the old man went on a trip. One day, a citizen of Tehran was a guest in his house and the conversation turned into a discussion about Tajrish and the large plane tree there. The old man admitted that he had planted that plane tree, and because of the woman's prayer, he and the tree would live for a thousand years.

Siyah Galesh [Black Cowherd]

This is the name of a cowherd in a forest who is a semi-savage and does not associate with people. He has a herd of wild cattle, and where he lives is known for being a sanctuary for animals, in which no animal must be harmed or hunted. If anyone dares to be impudent, Siyah Galesh will reward them with what they deserve. It has often been seen that hunters who did not heed his advice have gone there and in the morning their corpses were found, or when someone had harmed an animal, he would end up living in misery. It is also a popular belief that on Friday

---

[9] *Karnameh-ye Ardeshir Papakan*, pp. 32-44; Ferdowsi's *Shahnameh*, 4th printing, Khavar Publishers, pp. 104-114.

bazaar day, Siyah Galesh assumes the shape of an old man and sells butter. The butter purchased from him never finishes, but continuously increases; however, if the person who has bought it reveals to anyone that his butter increases or that it is from Siyah Galesh, his butter container will go dry immediately.

The City of Neyriz
There is a popular story about Plato, when he was asked by his students whether there was any medicine that restores life to a dead person. Plato gives them some instruction that, after his death, they should mix certain medicines, extract their oil, and then take his corpse to a bathhouse and rub his body with that oil to bring him back to life. After Plato's death, his students take his body to the bathhouse and follow his instructions. At the moment when he is regaining consciousness, there is a voice from the unknown, saying "*nariz*" [don't pour], while Plato is saying, "*beriz*" [pour]. In the middle of all this, the ceiling of the bathhouse collapses. The ruins of that bathhouse are in the city of Neyriz. Once a year, the voices can be heard saying, "nariz, beriz."

Murchehkhor [Anteater]
It is said that when the army of Islam arrived in Murchehkhor, the ants were ordered to eat the army of the infidels.[10]

Mazandaran
The Commander of the Faithful, Ali, ate food and shook his supper cloth in Mazandaran. That is why it is bountiful.

Kashan
There is a popular story that when Malek Ashtar wanted to build Hell, he asked for the hottest place on earth. They told him it was Kashan. To torment people, he ordered all the scorpions and snakes to be assembled in that city. However, he did not live long enough to complete the task. That is why there are a lot of snakes and scorpions in Kashan.

---

[10] As one of my friends says, this is a sign of "inferiority complex." See *Isfahan Nesf-e Jahan*, first printing, p. 15.

Kiga

The people of Kiga (a village along the road from Farahzad to Imamzadeh Davud) are cross-eyed and their eyes look to the left. The reason is that when Imamzadeh Davud was fleeing, he told them not to show where he was going to the enemy. When the infidels arrived and asked them, the people of Kiga did not tell them where he was. They only looked to the left, and their eyes stayed that way.

The Story of Shahrbanu

When Bibi Shahrbanu fled the infidels and reached the region of Rey, she was riding Zoljanah [Imam Hoseyn's horse] and her daughter Bibi Zobeydeh, who was sitting behind her on the saddle, was pregnant. On the road, people were surprised and sang the following verse:

Oh God, I fear my thinking has gone wild
The mother is a virgin, yet her daughter is with child

When the infidels got closer, Shahrbanu told Zobeydeh, "You are from the family of the Prophet [Mohammad]. No one would dare to touch you. You, get off the horse so Zoljanah can go faster." Zobeydeh got off the horse, and Shahrbanu fled until she reached the mountain. Thinking that she had been nearly caught by the enemy, she remembered her husband's advice, when he told her, "Whenever the infidels get close to you, say 'O God [*Ya Hu*], rescue me!' By mistake, however, she said, 'O mountain [*Ya kuh*], rescue me!'" At that very moment, the mountain opened its mouth and Sharhbanu rode into it with the horse. Only a bit of her veil got caught outside. The infidels arrived and saw the piece of the veil, but since it was near sunset, they marked the place and decided to come back on the following day to split the rocks. But on the following day, by the power of God, the entire mountain had become a collection of three rocks atop three rocks, and the infidels could not find the place they had marked. When pilgrims go to Bibi Shahrbanu's shrine, still today, they make a wish and place three stones, stacked up on top of each other.

When the infidels returned, a woman and her husband had become the custodians of the place where Bibi Shahrbanu had disappeared. The woman custodian received a message from the Unknown that on every Friday eve, she should place a pot of clean water, a bath towel, and a cake of soap behind the shrine without anyone knowing about it. The woman did as she was told. The next morning, she found a fistful of silver money on the towel. She picked up the money, repeated what she had done every Friday eve, and lived on that money. The woman had a son for whom she found a wife and arranged their wedding. At the time of her death, the woman told her daughter-in-law to place a pot of water and a bath towel behind the shrine every Friday eve. After her death, the daughter-in-law continued doing so; however, one Friday eve, her husband arrived and learned about her secret. In the middle of the night, she and her husband stood behind the door of the shrine while Bibi Shahrbanu was bathing. Bibi Shahrbanu realized that there was a man behind the door. Then, the husband and wife heard a voice that said, "Become blind not to see me!" The man immediately became blind. The woman continued doing what she was supposed to do, and apparently, she is still alive. Hence, men must not enter the shrine of Bibi Shahrbanu.

Green Dome

This is a shrine located in the Ark neighborhood of Mashhad where dervishes, opium smokers, and hashish smokers assemble. It is said that a person by the name of Mo'men [Faithful] is buried there, and the dervishes are fully devoted believers in that place. One of the hashish smokers has composed the following line about that celestial place:

"Hashish-land of Mashhad is the Green Dome, oh Faithful!"

Harun Valayat

This is an old tomb in Isfahan in which, apparently, a Jew is buried, and it is respected by common people. The poet Mokarram-Esfahani composed a poem about it, of which here are a few verses:

O Harun Velayat, perform your flaming miracle, I say
Take the mud-brick under his head where
*   Molla Nasir lay*
Alone in his grave, and turn it into baked brick,
This river is a mine of pebbles, come along and fix it
Because I am Harun Velayat, because I am a thug
*   and a lout*

> *That miraculous goat in the Paqal'eh neighborhood*
> *was let out*[11]
> *O Harun Velayat, turn that little goat into*
> *a camel of mine*
> *See that woman strolling flirtatiously around your shrine*
> *Stick a fistful of chickpea flour in the corner of*
> *her chador that's turned out*
> *Because I am Harun Velayat, because I am a thug*
> *and a lout*

Taq-e Ali [Ali's Arch]

This is a place near Kerman where, on the top of a mountain, there is a large stone carving of the name "Ali." At the foot
of the mountain, there is a spring and an ancient tree on which
people have hung candelabras and tied wish rags. A popular belief is that Ali had passed through that place and cut the mountain in half with his sword.

Sang-e Siyah [Black Stone]

There is a stone known by this name near the city of Mara-
gheh, under which women pass in order to get pregnant. If their
wish is fulfilled, that stone begins to quiver on its own.

Hanging Chain

In Tabriz, in an Imamzadeh shrine in the Charandab neighborhood, there is a hanging chain. Women make a wish and pull
on that chain. When they let go of the chain, if they begin to
spin, their wish will be fulfilled.

Ab-e Mahi [Fish Pond]

The tomb of Sa'di is an attraction for the people of Shiraz.
There is a *qanat* [aqueduct] there, the water of which is believed
to have many beneficial properties. It nullifies black magic, and
bathing in it is a favorite activity of common people.

---

[11] There used to be a goat in Isfahan called the Paqal'eh goat, the horns
of which they had gilded, and it was very much respected, such that it
could freely enter any house. It was rumored that it had taken shelter in
the shrine.

Allah-o Akbar Narrow City Gate

This is a holy place for the people of Shiraz. On the first day of every month, all the people need to go through it under a copy of the Koran above the gate, which is said to weigh 17 stones, and each page of which also weighs 17 stones.[12]

Mortaz Ali's Well [The Well of Ascetic Ali]

There is a grave in Shiraz which is in a ditch. To get one's wish and for health, people go there on Wednesday eves. There is a boiling pot there and a rock next to the wall on which they rub a prayer stone. If the prayer stone sticks to the rock, their wish will be fulfilled.

Baba Kuhi

This is [a tomb in a cave] located in Shiraz. It is believed that anyone who plays a musical instrument there will be harmed.

---

[12] A person who has seen that Koran says that it was transcribed by Hasan ibn Buyeh (for this reason, they attribute it to Imam Hasan), and its weight is no more than three or four stones.

21

Common Folk Myths

Gav-e Zamin [Bull of the Earth]: Earth is on the horn of the bull.[1] The bull stands on the fish, and when it gets tired, it shifts Earth from one horn to the other, and this causes earthquakes.

"Some have stated that Earth is on one horn of the bull, and whenever the bull gets tired, it moves its head, shakes it, and tosses the Earth onto its other horn, and any part of the Earth that lands on the horn of the bull will have an earthquake."[2]

> *Coupled with the Pleiades, in the sky there is a bull*
> *Hiding beneath the Earth, yet another bull*
> *If you are astute, open your eyes to the truth*
> *Below and above those two bulls are none but donkeys,*
> *forsooth*
> Omar Khayyam
> *Sunk into the fish and up into the moon it went*
> *The tip of the spear and the top of the royal tent*
> Ferdowsi
> *Am I the Bull of the Earth to lift the world, this one?*
> *Or the fourth firmament to haul about the Sun?*
> Mo'ezzi

The galaxy shows the way to Mecca.[3]

---

[1] The Greeks believe that Earth is on the shoulders of Atlas. In Aryan myths, the bull symbolizes power and energy, and it is regarded as sacred.

[2] *Majma' al-Nureyn*, p. 250.

[3] A collection of stars that looks spread out like a straw line and is known as a galaxy. According to Greek mythology, the galaxy is a pathway to the palace of Jupiter. The people of Siam consider the galaxy the "white elephant road." The Spanish regard it as the "road to Santiago," and the Turks believe that it is the "path of the pilgrims."

Qows-e Qazah [Rainbow]: *Nowseh, ranginkaman, kaman-e azfandak*, and the bow of Ali's bow and arrow are its other Persian names. In his book *Al-Hend*, Abu Reyhan Biruni states: "The Indians consider the rainbow as Indra's bow in the same way that common people call it Rostam's bow." Abu al-Faraj Runi has said:

Like a sword, the Sun your resolve it did forego
And there upon the cloud does weep Rostam's bow

Whenever the redness of the bow is excessive, it is a sign of bloodshed. If it is excessively green, it is the sign of a pleasant life, and if its yellowness is too much, it is the sign of illness. If when viewing it, one removes the head cover, it will make the hair thick.[4]

Rain: Every drop of rain is accompanied by an angel. There is an angel in the sky who has one thousand hands, and each hand has a million fingers. That angel is assigned to count the drops of rain.[5]

Asman Ghorreh [Thunder]: God orders the angels to drive the clouds away. The angels use whips to lash the clouds and the clouds roar. When there is lightning accompanied by thunder, it is from the whips of the angels. According to another version, it is God who is whipping the angels, who cry. According to yet another version, angels are riding chariots on the clouds.

Tir-e Shahab [Shooting Stars]: When Satan rubs his heels together, *al-khannas* [retreating devils] fall off his heels. These retreating devils get on one another's shoulders and go to the Seventh Heaven to see what is happening. God commands that one of them be shot, and then they all fall down.

---

[4] "It is the reflection of Mount Qaf, which consists of seven peaks, each of which is a colorful gem. Hence, if the redness of the rainbow is dominant, it symbolizes murder and war, and if green is dominant, it symbolizes low prices, and if yellowness is dominant, illness will dominate." *Jannat al-Kholud*

[5] The Arabic-speaking Iranian poet, Abu Nuwas, who made fun of this idea, was excommunicated by the Arabs, because, while drinking wine, he would hold his goblet under the rain and say that he wanted angels to enter his wine.

Venus: "She was a prostitute who had learned magic from [the two fallen angels] Harut and Marut, and with the power of sorcery and witchcraft, she went to the sky, where God metamorphosed her into Venus."[6]

Nurbaran [Shower of Light]: These are indisputable evidence fireballs around the shrines of Imamzadehs who go to visit one another. At the time when it happens, every wish will be fulfilled.

Moon and Sun: Moon is a male, and Sun is a female.[7] Moon said to Sun, "You should come out at night so the eyes of strangers do not see you." Sun said, "If anyone looks at me, I will hit his eyes with my hair." One day Moon had needles in his hand and wanted to make love to Sun. Sun's hair hit Moon's eyes and he became blind. Moon tossed the needles at Sun's face. From then on, it has not been possible to look at Sun, because she hits the eyes with needles.

Solar and Lunar Eclipse: Solar and lunar eclipses happen because a dragon is holding the sun and the moon in its mouth.[8] In order to scare the dragon and make it throw the moon or the sun up, people need to set off fireworks, play musical instruments, shoot arrows, and beat flat copper tubs with utensils. That will scare the dragon and release the moon or the sun. If during an eclipse, the moon or the sun turns purple, there will be bloodshed that year.

Gowhar-e Shabcheragh [Night-Glowing Pearl]: This is a precious gem that shines in the dark. It is the size of a chicken egg that is in the nose of a cow that lives in the sea. At night, the

---

[6] Mirza Aqa Khan Kermani, *Seh Maktub*.

[7] In popular songs, the Sun is addressed as "Lady Sun": *Lady Sun shone bright*. See *Owsaneh*, 1st printing, p. 3.

[8] *Right now seek my mother's reward, indeed*
Since from the dragon, the moon was freed
        From *Vis and Ramin*.
The coppersmith boy, with charcoal dust covering face and lips
The banging copper sound to the sky is thrust to mark the lunar eclipse
        Fathali Shah.

cow comes to the land and blows its nose, and the night-glowing pearl falls out of its nose, and it grazes in its light. Close to morning, the cow draws the pearl back up into its nose and returns to the sea.

Bakhtak [Succubus]: Bakhtak, also known as Faranjak, was a female slave who belonged to Alexander. When a crow pecked at a sheepskin full of the Water of Life and it spilled on the ground,[9] Bakhtak arrived, gathered a fistful of the water and drank it. Alexander became angry and ordered her nose to be cut off and replaced with a clay nose. This Bakhtak knows where treasures are hidden. When a person has a nightmare, it is Bakhtak who lies down on the top of that person. The sleeping person should try to grab Bakhtak's nose in the dark. Fearing the loss of her nose, Bakhtak reveals the hiding place of the treasure,[10] but as soon as the person tries to move his fingers, the nightmare ends. In other words, Bakhtak flees.

Ghul-e Biabani [Ghoul of the Desert]: This is a demon who lives in the mountains and deserts away from inhabited places, can assume any shape it wants, and kidnaps people. He licks the soles of the feet of a person sleeping in the desert and drinks his blood until he dies.

Some Devils: "The most famous among them is the ghoul. It is said that if a person is traveling and is alone at night in the desert, the ghoul will assault and kill him; and it is said that when devils eavesdrop, Almighty God repels them by burning them. Some burn, some fall into the sea and become Leviathans, and some go to the desert and become ghouls... And those who have seen a ghoul say that from its head to its navel, it is human-like, and from the navel down, the rest of it looks like a horse, and its hooves, like that of a donkey. One of the Companions of the Prophet said he saw a ghoul on his travels to the Levant. And it is reported and well known that the ghouls are demons that take the form of women, and there are many of them in the

---

[9] This is a reference to Alexander's travel to the Realm of Darkness and bringing the Water of Life.
[10] Idiom: "If you grab his nose, it will suck the life out of him."

woodlands, and if one of them gains victory over a person, it plays with him like a cat playing with a mouse, and if it sees that the person has a beautiful face, it becomes enchanted and molests him."[11]

Davalpa: This is an old man who sits at the side of the road crying and begging every passerby to pick him up and carry him across the stream of water. When a person picks him up, suddenly, a three-yard leg sticks out of his belly like a snake and wraps around the person, and Davalpa's arms also hold him tightly, and he orders the person to work and give the money to Davalpa. In order to get rid of Davalpa, get him drunk.[12]

"In the book, *Ajayeb al-Behar*, it is quoted from Ya'qub ibn Eshaq, who said: I was on Sagsaran [Dog-Eat-Dog] Island. I saw many trees. I went closer. I saw people with beautiful faces sitting under those trees. I sat down nearby. We did not speak each other's language. One of them placed his arm around my neck; and before I knew it, he was sitting on my neck and wrapping his legs around me and inciting me, and I decided to drop him from my neck. He scratched my face with his nails. I was walking around and picking and eating the fruits of those trees, and he also ate some fruit of the trees and tossed them to his companions, who ate them. I dropped him under the trees, and a branch stuck into his eyes and blinded him. I took some grapes and found a stone in a ditch and used it to express the juice. I gestured to him to drink it and he became drunk. His legs loosened, and I dropped him and was freed from that place."[13]

Harut and Marut:[14] "It is reported from the Messenger of God that the angels saw the rebellion of the offspring of Adam

---

[11] *Ajayeb al-Makhluqat*, p. 76.
[12] See the tales of Sindbad's voyages in *One Thousand and One Nights*.
[13] *Ajayeb al-Makhluqat*.
[14] "Harut and Marut are the names of two idols that were worshipped in ancient times by the people of Armenia. In the writings of historians, the names of these two worshipped idols in Armenian pronunciation are Hurut and Murut. One Armenian writer states:
'Of course, Hurut and Murut were the gallants of Oghri Tagh and Aminabigh, or perhaps another goddess which is still unknown to us as to whether they were assistants of the goddess, Spandaramet. They

and said, 'Do they not have the slightest understanding of the greatness of God?' The Lord Almighty said, 'If you were in the same situation as they are, you would also commit sin.' They said, 'How can this be? We praise You.' The Lord Almighty told them to choose two angels, and He sent them to earth, instilled in them human lust, and sinning came forth in them. Then, He gave them a choice between punishment in this world or the next world. One of them consulted the other and asked, 'What is your opinion?' The other said, 'Punishment in this world has an end but punishment in the next world does not.' Hence, they chose punishment in this world. There is another report by Ibn Abbas that states that Harut and Marut are chained together upside down in a well in the land of Babylon until Resurrection Day. Still another report states that the Lord Almighty told them, 'I send you both as messengers to the people and not to me.' He sent them to earth and told them to avoid heathenism, murder, theft, and adultery. Ka'b al-Ahbar says that not one day had passed before all four sins were committed by them."

Khar-e Dajjal [The Imposter's Donkey]: Dajjal has a saddle that he sews every night, and in the morning, it is ripped apart. On the day that the world comes to an end, the Imposter's Donkey will come out of a well in Isfahan. Each of its hairs plays a different musical instrument. Pastry falls out of its ears,

---

were the exuberant adjutants and good discoverers of the earth.' And in the desert, it must become known that Spandaramet was that goddess who was also worshipped in Iran in ancient times, because the Zoroastrians considered her to be the spirit of the earth and assumed that she makes all good plants grow from the soil. The people of Armenia regarded Aminabigh the god of vineyards and regarded Hurut and Murut the assistants of the spirit of the earth, because they thought of them as spirits that knew about the winds and would make the winds to provide the clouds that bring rain and strike the clouds on the top of the high mountain that they called Oghri Tagh to rain on the earth... In old books of the people of India and also of the Maratha, they are often mentioned, and Indians considered them to be the gods of storms and strong winds." *Yana Bei' al-Islam*, pp. 86-88.

and its droppings are dates. Following it will send a person to Hell.[15]

"Worse than all donkeys is Dajjal's Donkey, which that cursed one rides on the day he appears. The color of that donkey is red. Its forelegs and hind legs are blue, and its head is as big as a huge mountain, and its behind is as large. Every step that it takes is nearly six *parasang*s. This was according to *Zobdat al-Ma'aref*. People can hear music from the donkey's hair. Its droppings look like figs and dates. Dajjal himself is twenty yards in height. He has two eyes on the top of his head, and the slits of his eyes are very long. He is blind in one eye. He has a long pockmarked face."[16]

Nasnas [Humanoid Demon]: These are demons that resemble humans, which consist of half of a human body lengthwise. They leap on one leg, and their language is Arabic.[17]

"There are abundant numbers of *nasnas*es in Aden and Oman. This is an animal that resembles a human and has one arm, one leg, and one eye, and its arm is on its chest. It speaks Arabic, and people hunt and eat it.[18] This is verified by what the learned erudite Imam Zakariya ibn Mohammad ibn Mahmud Qazvini mentions about *nasnas* in *Asar al-Belad*, in which he states: 'Shihr is a region between Aden and Oman on the seashore. Ambergris from Shihr is related to it, because ambergris is found on those coasts, and there are many forests there in which *nasnas*es exist.' An Arab told an anecdote: 'I entered Shihr and stayed at the home of a notable. Then I asked him about *nasnas*es. He said, "We hunt them and eat them. It is an animal like one half of a human and it has one arm and one leg. Also its other parts are half of those of a human." I said that I would like to see it. He then told his servants to hunt a *nasnas* for us. On the following day, they brought one. Its face was like that of a human, except that it had half of a face, and it had one arm on its

---

[15] There is a well in an herb and spice shop in the Ancient Square in Isfahan that is known as Dajjal's Well.
[16] *Majma' al-Nureyn*, p. 219.
[17] There are references to half-humans in folktales and also in the *Bundahishn*.
[18] *Ghiyas ol-Loghat*.

chest and also one leg. When it saw me, it said in Arabic, "*Ana bellah wa bek*," which means, "I take refuge in God and in you." I told them to let it go free. They said that I should not heed what it said because it was their food. But I did not give up and was persistent until they released it, and it fled as fast as the wind and escaped. When my host came back, he said to his servants, "Didn't I tell you to hunt something for us?" They replied, "We did, but your guest let it go free." He laughed and said, "I swear to God that it deceived you." And he ordered his servants to go hunting on the following day. They did, and they took the dogs with them. I was also with them. Late at night, we arrived in a forest. I suddenly heard someone say in Arabic, "Hey, Abu Mejmar. Morning is bright and night has ended. Hurry into the shelter!" Another responded, "Eat and don't fear." Then the servants set the dogs after them, and I saw two dogs hanging on Abu Mejmar... However, the two dogs captured it; and when the host was ready as was his custom, they brought the roasted Abu Mejmar.' Also, Ibn al-Keys al-Nomri told an anecdote and said: 'We were in a caravan and lost our way and ended up traveling in a forest by the side of the sea, neither ends of which were visible. Suddenly, I saw a tall old man who looked like a date palm tree with half of a head and body, one eye, and one leg who was running like a horse and reciting Arabic poetry.'"[19]

Ya'juj and Ma'juj [akin to Gog and Magog]: These are people who are short, with ears as big as those of elephants that drag on the ground. This species caused chaos in the world. Alexander Dhul-Qarnayn [Owner of Two Horns] built a strong barrier wall in front of them to prevent them from getting out. That barrier is made of seven molten metals. The width of the wall is equivalent to 7,000 years of traveling. What Ya'juj and Ma'juj do from evening to morning is lick the wall of the barrier. Near morning, this thick wall becomes as thin as a hair; but just then, they become sleepy, and the wall once again becomes as thick as it was.[20]

---

[19] Extracted from *Kaveh* magazine, new edition, vol. 1, nos. 4 and 5, p. 6.
[20] According to Hamzeh-Esfahani, Esfandiyar built a wall to stop the Turks.

"Ya'juj and Ma'juj, this is a tribe the number of whose members only God knows, and their bodies resemble those of humans, and they are mean and antagonistic, like ferocious animals. One of them alone gives birth to many, and they live on things that fall from the sea to the shore... Another are the Mansek, and they are a tribe to the west near Ya'juj and Ma'juj, whose ears are like the ears of elephants, each ear the size of a kilim, one can be like a carpet and the other like a quilt."[21]

Jabalqa and Jabalsa: "It is reported that God created two cities, one in the east and the other in the west, and the one in the east is Jabalqa and the one in the west is Jabalsa,[22] and each city has 12,000 city gates, and the distance between one gate and the next is one *parasang*. Those cities are so crowded that each gate has 10,000, and also they never get their turn, and if there were not so many people in the east and the west, every night when the sun sank into that spring and in the morning when it came up, all the people of the world would hear, but because of the noise and hubbub of those cities, they cannot hear the rising sun, and those people are all faithful, and those who are in the city in the east are the remnants of the tribe of Ad, who were converted by the Prophet Hud, and those who are in the west are from the tribe of Samud, who were converted by the Prophet Saleh, and behind that city there are three nations, one of which is called Mansek, the second one Tafil, and the third one is called Taris. After all these, Ya'juj and Ma'juj did not convert on the night of Me'raj [the Prophet Mohammad's ascension to Heaven]; but the residents of Jabalqa and Jabalsa converted. The three tribes that reside further behind Jabalqa and Jabalsa remained as infidels."[23]

According to "Sudgar Nask," Kaykavus built seven structures,[24] one made of gold, two made of silver, two made of steel,

---

[21] *Ajayeb al-Makhluqat.*

[22] *When you speak based on religion, whether it be in Syriac*
When you seek a place for God, whether Jabalqa or Jabalsa
                    Sana'i

[23] *History of Tabari.*

[24] The number seven is of special significance, and we see it in all sorts of old legends and tales. In tales we find seven iron shoes, seven iron canes, seven heavens, seven days of the week, seven colors, seven

and two made of crystal, and he imprisoned the demons of Mazandaran in this fortress, so that by this means, he could prevent
their evil deeds. These seven structures were enchanted, because
they would take anyone who became old, feeble, and close to
death around these fortifications, which restored their earlier
strength and they became a fifteen-year-old person. In the Iranian *Bundahishn* published by Anklesaria, on page 210, it is stated
that Kaykavus's place was a golden palace, which was his own
residence, and two crystal houses were for his horses, and two
steel ones for his herds and cattle. It also states in Pahlavi:

"And whatever is tasted from it and also (anyone who tasted
that spring) the spring makes one deathless. If a person who has
been enfeebled by years, in other words, an old man, enters it, he
will come out of the other end a fifteen-year-old young man, and
death will flee from him."[25]

Gang Dez [or, *Gang Dezh*, meaning, Gang Fortress]: In
Pahlavi narratives, in the *Bundahishn* and the Yashts [Avestan
hymns] (51-54), it is stated that this fortress is located in the
north among the mountains, and the river "Chehrmiyan" passes
through it, and it is where Khorshidchehr, one of Zoroaster's
sons, lives. This ever-spring fortress was built on the heads of
demons. Kaykhosrow, however, solidified it on the ground and
built seven walls, one of gold, and one each of silver, steel,
brass, iron, crystal, and precious stones, and there are roads there
the length of which are 700 *parasang*s and it has 15 gates, such
that if they want to travel from one gate to the next, it takes 22
days in spring.

With a slight change, narratives about the seven walls state:
"one of stone, one of steel, one of ruby, and so on. There are 14
mountains in the fortress and seven rivers pass through it, and
the land is so arable that whenever a donkey urinates on it, on the
same night, plants grow as high as the height of a human. Each
one of these 15 gates are as high as the height of 50 men, and the
distance between these gates is 700 *parasang*s. Siyavash built

domes of Bahram, seven feats of Rostam, seven items with S in the
Haft Sin, seven daughters, seven stars, seven countries, and so on.
[25] This is not dissimilar to the myth of the Realm of Darkness and Alexander's quest for the Water of Life.

Gang Dezh on 'Kamar' in the memory of the Kayanians. Kaykhosrow took possession of it, and that king became *pashutan* [invincible] and deathless, and old age and feebleness were erased from him. The people of Gang Dezh live happily. They are devout and pious, and they will not return to Iranshahr unless Pashutan is their guide to incite them against the enemies of Iranshahr, and in this way on Resurrection Day, he will provide great help in the victory and dominance of Ohrmazd and Ameshaspands over the demons."[26]

It appears that Gang Dez is analogous to Kaykavus's fortress on Mount Alborz, which is the same as Mount Qaf of legends and tales.

Mount Qaf: "Mount Qaf is an emerald in (the middle of) the world, and the world consists of two plains and a mountain. On the right of the mountain is the plain of black Africans, which is the tropical plain; on the left of that mountain is the cold plain of narrow-eyed cannibal Turks; and the middle of this mountain is the place of fairies."[27]

"It is stated in *Ara'es al-Majales* on pages 7 and 8: Almighty God created a huge mountain made of green topaz to which belongs the green of the sky. They call it Mount Qaf. And then it is surrounded by all the earth, and this is that which God has sworn by and said in the glorious Koran, in 'Qesas al-Anbia' [Stories of the Prophets] (p. 5), that one day Abdollah ibn Salam asked His Holiness Mohammad, 'What is above the earth?' He answered, 'Mount Qaf.' He asked, 'What is Mount Qaf made of?' He said, 'Of green emerald, and the greenness of the sky is from that.' He asked, 'How far is it to the top of Mount Qaf?' He said, 'Five hundred years of travel.' He asked, 'How long does it take to go around it?' He said, 'Two thousand years of travel.'"[28]

Dragon: Croesus' Treasure, which consisted of seven royal casks,[29] sank into the ground and its guard is the dragon that sleeps on them.

---

[26] [Arthur] Christensen, *Les Kayanides*.

[27] From the hand-written manuscript of *Salaman and Absal*.

[28] *Yana Bei' al-Islam*, p. 111.

[29] *Even Croesus with all his forty houses of treasure perished.* Sa'di.

"The dragon is a huge beast, a frightful sight, with a wide mouth and many teeth, bright eyes, and it is long. Early on, it used to be a snake, and as time has passed, it has become a dragon and changed shape. As has been stated: '*With time, the snake will learn that into a dragon it will turn.*' The author of *Ajayeb al-Makhluqat* states that when a snake reaches the length of 30 yards and is 100 years old, it is called a dragon, and it gradually becomes bigger and bigger, until it reaches such a size that the land animals become desperate in its presence, and Almighty God tosses it into the sea, and its body in the sea grows such that its upper part reaches 10,000 yards; it grows two fins like the fish, and its movement causes waves; and since its harm also spreads in the sea, Almighty God tosses it to the land of Ya'juj and Ma'juj to become their food. We should surmise the good character of the Ya'juj and Ma'juj tribe from the fact that since all the components of their beings are from such a peaceful animal, inevitably, they are such nice characters. Eating the heart of the dragon increases bravery. Mesmerized animals become its food. If they wrap its skin around a person in love, his love will fade away. Wherever they bury its head, the conditions will improve in that place."[30]

"The dragon is a large snake and its name is the epithet of Zahhak. The author says that they used to call Zahhak *Ezhdaha* [Dragon]. It has been written that he was raised in Babylon, learned sorcery, and showed his face as a dragon to his father, who wanted to prevent him from engaging in sorcery. A demon who was his teacher told him, 'If you want me to teach you sorcery, kill your father.' He killed his father and shed a great deal of unjust blood, and he was called *Ezhdaha*. Arabs called him *Ezdehaq* and Arabicized it to Zahhak."[31]

Qoqnos [Phoenix]: "It is known to be in India. It has a long beak with many holes out of each of which a different song comes. When it trills, no bird can resist its singing. It does not reproduce and is androgynous. At the time of departure, it flaps its wings countless times, because of which its wings ignite into a fire and flame up, and both wings burn, and when rain falls on

---

[30] *Nozhat al-Qolub*, p. 146.
[31] *Anjomanara Dictionary.*

the ashes, a worm appears that feeds on the ashes to grow and become another phoenix. The instrument of the organ was invented on the basis of the singing of that bird."[32]

"Qoqnos is a bird in India. It gathers a great deal of firewood for building its nest, and it rubs its beak on the beak of the female, which ignites a fire and both burn, and then when it rains on their ashes, they both reappear and spread their wings from the ashes."[33]

"And they say that the angel that pulls the chariot of the sun is in the form of a horse by the name of Alus,[34] but Alus is that horse that pulls the sky, and they say that it is farsighted and from a place far away it can hear the sound of the hooves of the horses, and it is most patient but cannot tolerate cold regions, and having it is auspicious, however, it is delicate."[35]

Samandar [Salamander]: This is a well-known animal that does not burn in fire, and some have said that it resides in fire, and when it comes out of the fire, it dies; and some have considered it to look like a rat, and some, capable of flying, which is also called salamander... In *Tohfeh*, it states that it is an animal similar to the snake, and it has arms and legs, but its arms are short, and it is slow moving, and its color is yellow and black, and its tail is short; and they have tested that its skin does not burn in fire and fire has no effect on it, and if they drop it into a burning clay bread oven, it diminishes the fire, and one *mesqal* of it is a lethal poison. Extremely warm, dry, and epispastic, its skin is foul-smelling, and its antidote is turtle egg. It is called *ilan aq veran* in Turkish, and its Greek name is *salamándra*, and its popular name in Persian is derived from that.[36]

Uj ibn Onoq: This was a very tall man who would take out a fish from the sea, roast it in front of the sun, and eat it. One day

---

[32] *Nozhat al-Qolub*. This legend was taken from the Greek legend of the phoenix, and the word *qoqnos* is also based on the word for phoenix.

[33] *Ajayeb al-Makhluqat.*

[34] *Nowruznameh*, p. 51.

[35] Also see *Ajayeb al-Makhluqat.*

[36] *Anjomanara Dictionary.*

he felt arrogant, and boasting, he said, "There is no creature taller than me." When it was time for him to hunt, he reached out into the sea and grabbed a fish by the middle, pulled it out, and held it against the sun. When he looked, he saw that the head and tail of the fish were still in the sea. He was frightened and let go of the fish.[37]

Simorgh: "It is stated in *Ajayeb al-Makhluqat* that Simorgh is such a strong bird that it can easily snatch an elephant, and they have called it the king of birds, because it hunts for its own survival and leaves the rest for other animals, and it does not return to what it has partly eaten. This is the character of kings. And it is said that it lives for 1,700 years, and after 300 years it lays an egg, and the chick hatches after 25 years. It is stated in Kolayni's commentary on the Koran that Anqa [Arabic for Simorgh and Phoenix] initially lived among the people and harmed the people, until during the time of the Prophet Hantaleh, it kidnapped a bride with all her clothes and ornaments. The Prophet prayed, 'Oh God, take it and cut off its offspring and cast upon it pestilence.' God Almighty sent a fire to burn it, and nothing remained of it but a name."[38]

Following this introduction, the author of *Nozhat al-Qolub* provides a series of strange, odd, and fabricated information about Simorgh that is not worthy of mention. However, that which is popular among the people is that in Iranian legends, there are two Simorghs. One was the tutor and guardian of Rostam, and the other, a large bird that was killed by Esfandiyar. According to the *Shahnameh*, the first Simorgh had its nest on Mount Alborz (Mount Qaf) far away from the people and did not associate with people, and during its flight, the air would turn dark and black. When Zal was born, his father, Sam, ordered his son to be placed on the road. Simorgh took Zal to its nest, raised him, and tutored him. Since Simorgh was capable of speech, it taught Zal how to speak. Later on, when it returned Zal to his

---

[37] Also see *Ajayeb al-Makhluqat*.
[38] From *Nozhat al-Qolub*.
Obsolete became honor, and annihilated became loyalty
Of both only their names remained, as did of Simorgh and Alchemy
     Abd al-Vase' Jabali

father, as it was about to fly away, it gave Zal a fistful of its feathers, so that whenever Zal felt that he needed Simorgh, or when he was at a loss as to what to do, he would burn one of those feathers.[39] Once, at the birth of the famed Rostam, and another time, during the battle between Rostam and the invincible Esfandiyar, Simorgh was summoned by burning its feather, and both times, Simorgh did not hesitate to provide consultation and assistance. In contrast to this Simorgh of good deeds, who is the king of birds,[40] there is also a demonic Simorgh, which Esfandiyar killed through a ruse during his seven feats, as is detailed in the *Shahnameh*.[41]

---

[39] *Toss one of my feathers on fire, I say*
My glamour you'll see, right away
        Ferdowsi
[40] *Shahnameh*, published in Florence, pp. 133, 139, 191, 222.
[41] Ibid., p. 1597.

22

Miscellaneous[1]

When a child is newly born, during the clipping of its fingernails, money needs to be placed in its shoes in order for the child to become wealthy, or they should place a pen in its hand for it to become an author.

If a pregnant woman sees a dead person, her child will have the evil eye.

If a pregnant woman is left alone from the time of delivery for ten days, she will be haunted by the jinn.

If a child gets sick and no medicine helps its recovery, it can be diagnosed as having become haunted by the jinn. They must take the child to a prayer-charm scribe to incant verses that drive away the jinn.

When a mother who has newly given birth enters a public bathhouse and another mother who has newly given birth enters the bathhouse at the same time, whichever one leaves the bathhouse later, her child will get sick, unless she takes the other woman by surprise and leaves the bathhouse sooner.

If the milk of a nursing mother is poured into some place that is dirty, her milk will dry up. Hence, the milk should be poured into running water, or in the shade, where the sun does not shine.

If the umbilical cord of a newborn is placed in a mouse hole, the child will become a troublemaker.

If a person wants her child to survive and grow up and not die, she should take a set of clothing from the child of a woman who has given birth to several children, none of whom have

---

[1] Since while this book was being printed, a number of utterances and topics were left out, and also I found some new topics, I am including them under this title.

died, and put them on her own child. That child will grow up and will not die prematurely.

If a person gathers breadcrumbs in the alleyway, her child will not die.

Placing a child on the wall shelf will shorten its life, and it will remain lethargic and scrawny.

One should not kiss the back of the neck of a child, because kissing it makes the child ill-tempered and stubborn.

If one hand of a child is kissed, the other one must also be kissed, otherwise the child will get sick.

When a child writhes, the child should be followed with a plant which is known as a climbing vine.

If an empty cradle is rocked, the child's ears will hurt.

If an infant is fed the milk that its own breast has produced, it will develop a good singing voice.

When a child grumbles while nursing, someone should say, "Boobie is a deaf mute." If they do not, the child will get sick.

When a child gets the runs from both ends (gets diarrhea and also vomits), aloeswood and male and female climbing vines are tied together and tossed on the roof.

A person carrying snakestones should not go into 40 days of seclusion near a child, because the child will be haunted.[2]

When a child steals something from its parents, God bursts out laughing.

When a non-seyyed wet nurse places her breast into the mouth of a seyyed child, her breast will not burn in Hell fire.

A child who is born in the seventh month of pregnancy will be hasty in everything.[3]

To change the name of a child, pottage must be cooked, and a group of people should be invited before the name change.

If a newborn is lethargic, throw its umbilical cord on fire. It will revive him.

Danduni: When a child's gums blister, people make *dan-duni* [teething pottage] for charity. Forty each of legumes, such as lentils, chickpeas, de-husked wheat, mung beans, red beans, and black-eyed peas, are counted in addition to as much as they

---

[2] Yemeni agate does the same.
[3] Idiom: "Were you born at seven months?"

can afford of the same legumes, and they are placed in a pot and boiled with some water, and they are steamed like plain steamed rice. Sometimes oil and sautéed onions are also added. (All of these are provided by the parents of the child. It is unlike religiously-pledged pottage, the ingredients of which must be panhandled.) Some of it is poured in front of pigeons at an Imamzadeh shrine.[4]

After the foreskin of a child is removed, it is put on a string and hung around the child's neck. After seven days, it is tossed in front of a rooster.

It is not good to visit a woman from the time of childbirth for ten days, unless she has a chador around her shoulders or the child is taken to another room.

If a person has been the target of the evil eye, alum is circled around that person's head, a special prayer is recited, and the alum is tossed on fire. If it becomes the shape of an eye, that person has been the target of the evil eye and will recover; if the shape is disorderly, the person is haunted by the jinn; and if it is the shape of a four-legged stool, the person will die and this stool is the coffin. Then the alum is placed in water and the person's forehead, palms, soles, and chest are marked with it. Then the water is poured into a bowl, and someone takes it and dumps it at the beginning of the alleyway, comes back, and says hello. A member of the household asks, "Where are you coming from?" The person answers, "From the house of the enemy." The member of the household asks, "What was he doing?" The other one answers, "He was in the throes of death." The response is, "I hope to God he will perish."

When traveling, if a thin, dark seyyed coincidentally travels with a person, it is not a good sign for the traveler. In contrast, if he coincidentally travels with a gypsy, it is auspicious.

When a traveler departs at an auspicious hour, it is a bad omen if he returns right away. People of villages in Khorasan Province refer to this as "*chapik*," and it is not good to *chapik*.

Pouring water and barley behind a departing traveler expedites his return.

---

[4] In villages, this pottage is one of their regular foods, which they call "*duni*." They call it "*danduni*" and perform these ceremonies only when a child is teething.

If a member of the household is traveling and a species of crows known as "*kalanjadak*" in Khorasan caws above that house, good news will come from the traveler.[5]

In the villages of Khorasan Province, when there is no rain, children organize a rally, place the head of a donkey on a stick, go to the door of every house, and say, "Donkey head, if you could, go and buy some firewood." In this way, they collect a large amount of firewood and burn the donkey head on the top of a mountain to get rain.

In Khorasan Province, when they want the rain to stop, they perform the ritual of "chaining the Koran," which means they drop a special talisman along with a copy of the Koran, cat and dog hair, bread, and human excrement into water to stop the rain. Sticking a "forty S talisman" on the wall also accomplishes the same.

In Mazandaran Province, the belief is that if upon leaving the house in the morning a woman is encountered, it is a bad omen.

Visiting a patient on Wednesday or Sunday eves is calamitous for the patient.

If a person gives away money on a Saturday, money will leave his pocket for an entire week. Conversely, when a person receives money on a Saturday, he will be rich for the entire week.

The arrival of a guest on a Wednesday eve is inauspicious. It is also a bad omen to visit someone's home on a Friday eve, since it will deprive the house of its Friday eve auspiciousness.

In Khorasan Province, to nullify the inauspiciousness of the last Wednesday eve of the Islamic lunar month of Safar, people must cook plain rice, light a fire on the roof of the house, shoot a rifle, and in an earthenware jug, place wild rue, salt, cotton seeds, unripe barley, and water and toss it on the ground from the roof.

On the eve of the 12th day of the Islamic lunar month of Sha'ban, or the first day of *Barat* [expurgation from sin], people cook halva and give it to beggars for the absolution of the souls

---

[5] In Mazandaran, many people have the same belief regarding a species of raven which, in Mazandarani dialect, they call "*ghashnik*," which is most likely a combination of *khosh* [happy] and *nik* [good].

of the dead. On the second night, they cook and give away egg-drop soup; and on the third night, they light each hallway to the rooms with oil lamps or candles, because on that night, the dead return to visit their own homes.

If anyone bakes cookies on the day of Ashura to eat in the mourning ceremonies, blood will be shed.

If a woman goes to the public bathhouse three or four times on Wednesdays, her husband will die.

It is a bad omen to clip fingernails and toenails and to do laundry on Wednesdays. Laundry should not be done on a Friday, because on Fridays, all waters move in the direction of Paradise, and they must not be contaminated.

Blessing is reduced if one sits at the corner of the supper cloth.

Lamps should not be placed in the form of a triangle.

Anyone who eats onions on forty-one consecutive Saturdays will become a Hajji.

Onions should not be eaten on Fridays, because they prevent angels from coming over one's head.

If someone borrows a pot or any black container from a neighbor and wants to bring it back at night, it should not be accepted, especially if there is an ill person in the house. It is also a bad omen to get water and fire from another house near sunset; and these two opposites, that are the source of the brightness of the house, should not be allowed to be taken out.[6]

If salt is sprinkled on the ground, a quarrel will ensue.

When buying salt from the grocer near sunset, one must ask for "*ta'am*" [food] and not mention the word salt, otherwise, the grocer will not give you salt.

One should not drink water at night while standing up.

---

[6] *Do not pour water out at night, O brother*
Since it is both toil and a crime, none other
One should not draw water from the well at night
Even if it is for a purpose that is right
Only draw water after reciting a prayer
With a bright lamp constantly placed there
Then one can sprinkle it or even drink it
If there is no purpose, do not even think it
      Darab Pahlan, *Farziyyatnameh*, pp. 19-20.

During the transition of the year at the vernal equinox, hookahs should not be touched.

Putting a hand under the chin brings misfortune. Crouching causes adversity.

A person whose brother is alive should not eat sheep eyes.

A person who does not eat meat for forty days is not a Muslim. A call for prayers should be recited into his ears.

If a person pours water into the firepit stove, he will be haunted by the jinn.

Holding the bristles of the broom toward the sky will result in a quarrel.

A gadfly sitting on a person will bring wealth for him.

A spider web is Satan's watchband.

Eating a ladybug (a small insect that is often seen among ruby grapes) makes the person welcome wolves.

If bread or water makes a person gag at the supper cloth, one of his relatives is hungry. If a piece of torn flatbread stands horizontally, a guest will arrive. If a dish moves, a member of the household is feeling offended. According to another version, a heavenly spirit is present at the supper cloth.

If a person is alone and gets scared, reciting the Koranic verse, "Allah is better at guarding and He is most merciful to those who show mercy" [Joseph, 64], four times and blowing around himself will drive away all disasters and the jinn.

If a person encounters a strong tornado, that person should say, "I seek refuge with Allah from the accursed Satan." The tornado will subside immediately.

If a person stands on a threshold and places his hands on both sides of the doorframe, a quarrel will ensue. To prevent a quarrel, he must clap his hands three times.

When lighting a fire, if the flames of the fire in the middle start to make a noise and it sizzles, it means that someone is talking behind the person's back.

When in a cloth weaving workshop the loom needs to be changed, if no more than one or two yards have been woven and someone in the household cuts that piece of canvas or fabric, he will either get sick or die. Hence, a stranger should cut it.

The cotton rolls that women prepare for spinning must definitely be completed by Friday eve. It is a bad omen for the people of the household to have any cotton rolls left on Saturday.

Cattle owners do not sell milk or yogurt to a person who wants to use it as an ointment for wounds. They say selling it will reduce the cow's milk.

Before burying a dead person, his coffin is placed on the ground and picked up three times to make the dead person familiar with his grave.

In some villages of Khorasan, if a white butterfly circles the house on a Friday eve, they say that the spirit of one of their relatives has come to visit.

When talking about bad wounds, such as the Aleppo boil, scrofula, and others, one should not point with his finger to any part of his own body, because he might get that wound.

To win in a game, gamblers urinate on their own hands.

When a person's mother is a seyyed, that person is called "*sharif*" [noble].

People swear on grains of rice and say, "I swear on these uncounted grains."

If wild rue is grown in the courtyard of a house, it will result in homeless exile.

Sprinkling water on a grave refreshes the soul of the dead.

If the dead person has done good deeds, a bright angel will appear to him in the grave, hold his hand, and take him to Paradise;[7] and if he has been a sinner, he will be taken to Hell with a fiery club.

It is a popular belief that each of the members of one of the families of the Qajar Turks has a small tail.

Every day, 1,000 people die and 1,000 people are born.

---

[7] In Zoroastrian books, there are detailed poetic accounts about a righteous and a sinful dead person. At the dawn of the fourth day, the righteous person smells a pleasant and mild breeze and a bright beautiful maiden appears before his eyes. The spirit of the dead person asks who she is in a surprised voice. She responds, "I am the result of your good words, good deeds, and good thoughts." The opposite of this happens to a dead sinner. (See: *Ardavizhnameh*, *Menog-i Khrad*, and *Denkard*). All that is related to supernatural issues and the life of the spirit after death, such as the Serat Bridge (Chinvat Bridge), the four-eyed dog in Hell (the golden-eared dog), and so on are astonishingly similar to the same issues in Zoroastrianism, the discussion of which in a different context would be most interesting.

God's rod of punishment makes no sound
When it strikes, no cure is found

Canopus: If this supergiant binary star shines on a girl's face, she will become beautiful and healthy. If it shines on fruit, it will become tasty and harmless, and will change color.

Explanatory Notes

Abd al-Vase' Jabali: A 12th century Persian poet who served at the court of the Ghaznavid king, Bahram Shah.

Abu Darda: Common people erroneously believe that the person buried in the tomb of Abu Darda was a companion of the Prophet Mohammad.

Abu Lo'lo': Also known as Baba Shoja'eddin, was a Persian slave of the governor of Baṣra and he assassinated the caliph Omar in 644 CE. While some reports indicate that he was killed as he was trying to escape, Iranians believe that his escape was successful and that he made his way back to Kashan. He is considered a hero for Iranian Shi'ites. For more, see: ABŪ LO'LO'A in *Encyclopedia Iranica* online.

Abu Mansur Tha'alibi: A 10th-11th century poet and writer of Arabic prose, Abu Mansur was born in Nishapur but was of Arab ethnicity. His original Arabic *Ghurar akhbar muluk al-Furs wa-siyarihim* is a history of pre-Islamic Persian dynasties.

Abu Nuwas: Regarded as a most important Abbasid Caliphate era poet, Abu Nuwas is best known for his "*khamriyyat*" or wine poetry.

Abu Reyhan Biruni: A 10th-11th century Persian polymath who was most highly regarded as an expert in many fields of knowledge, including astronomy, physics, geography, geodesy, pharmacology, mineralogy, history, anthropology, and philosophy, among others.

Ahman and Bahman: These are names given to two parts of winter, called *chelleh-ye bozorg* [big *chelleh*] and *chelleh-ye kuchek* [small *chelleh*]. In Persian folklore, Ahman and Bahman are considered brothers whose mother is Sarma Pir-e Zan [Old Woman Cold].

Ajayeb al-Makhlughat: The full title of this book is *Ajayeb al-Makhlughat wa Gharayeb al-Mowjudat* [Wonders of Creation and Oddities of Existing Beings], by Imam Zakariya ibn Mohammad ibn Mahmud Qazvini.

Al-Athar al-Baqiya: A reference to Abu Reyhan Biruni's *Kitab al-Athar al-Baqiyah an al-Qurun al-Khaliyah* [The Remaining Signs of Past Centuries], published in 1000 CE.

Al-Hamd: Refers to the first verse of the first chapter of the Koran, which means, "all praise is due to God, Lord of both worlds."

Ali: The cousin and son-in-law of the Prophet Mohammad, Ali ibn Abi Taleb was the fourth of the first caliphs who succeeded the Prophet. For Shi'ites, he is the first of their twelve imams who succeeded the Prophet Mohammad one after another. Among Shi'ites, he is most revered, and referred to with a variety of titles and names, including Morteza Ali and Commander of the Faithful, and he is one of the members of *Al-e Aba* [the People of the Cloak], who consisted of the Prophet Mohammad, his daughter Fatemeh, her husband Ali, and their two sons Hasan and Hoseyn. Ali is in particular greatly revered by most Sufi sects.

Allameh Helli: One of the most famous 13th-14th century Shi'ite religious jurists and polymaths, who authored hundreds of books on a variety of subjects, including theology, philosophy, history, and mathematics.

Amir Arsalan: Reference to a popular 19th century romance and adventure novel, *Amir Arsalan-e Namdar* [Renowned Amir Arsalan], which was told as a pre-bedtime story to Nasereddin Shah Qajar by his Royal Court storyteller, Naqibolmamalek, and was written down by the shah's daughter, Fakhrodowleh.

Anjomanara Dictionary: Also, *Farhang-e Anjomanara*, a 19th century Persian dictionary compiled by Rezaqoli Khan Hedayat.

Anklesaria: Behramgore Tehmuras Anklesaria (1873-1944) was a Parsi scholar who translated many works from Middle Persian into English.

Ardeshir Papakan: also known as Ardeshir I, was the founder of Sassanid Empire and ruled Persia from 211 to 224 AD.

Asar al-Belad: The full title of this work is *Asar al-Belad* va *Akbar al-Ebad* [Monuments of the Lands and Historical Traditions about Their Peoples] by Imam Zakariya ibn Mohammad ibn Mahmud Qazvini.

Ashab-e Kahf: The story of "Ashab-e Kahf" [Companions of the Cave] is told in the "Al-Kahf" Surah of the Koran.

Ash-e Reshteh: also known as "*ash-e barg*," is a thick vegetarian soup or pottage made with fresh herbs such as leeks and parsley, legumes including beans and chickpeas, and flour noodles.

Ashura: The 10th day of the Islamic lunar year of Moharram and the anniversary of the martyrdom of the third Shi'ite imam, Hoseyn, in the battle of Karbala in 680 CE.

Astir: A monetary unit. An *astir* during the Sassanid era was worth four dirhams. The weight measure *sir*, equivalent to 80 grams, which is now used is a derivative of *astir*.

Ayat Prayers: *Ayat* means "signs," and these signs refer to natural phenomena that frighten people, such as earthquakes, lunar and solar eclipses, and other fearsome natural incidents during which Muslims are obliged to perform special prayers.

Baba Shoja'oddin: See: Abu Lo'lo'.

Battle of Karbala: Occurred in the year 680, when the small army of the Prophet Mohammad's grandson, Hoseyn, fought against the much larger forces of the Omayyad caliph, Yazid I, during which 72 of Hoseyn's family members and supporters were killed. It is considered the most important event in Shi'ite history.

Bibi Hur: Bibi Nur and Bibi Hur are legendary figures who are thought to have been the daughters of a prophet or the sisters of the King of Fairies. Girls who want to see their future husbands in a dream place their shoes, stockings, and chadors under their pillows and think about the two Bibi sisters before falling asleep. Their banquet spreads arranged for this purpose must include flatbread, goat cheese, green herbs, a mirror, a bowl of date syrup, a bowl of yogurt, collyrium and collyrium applier, six types of *qavut*, and a lit candle.

Bibi Nur: See Bibi Hur.

Bibi Shahrbanu: There is a shrine on the slopes of Mount Rey in greater Tehran which is reputed to be of Bibi Shahrbanu, the daughter of the last Sassanid king, Yadegerd III, and the wife of Imam Hoseyn. Some scholars are of the opinion that this shrine was originally a temple to Anahita, a popular Zoroastrian deity of water.

Borhan-e Qate': Written by Mohammad Hoseyn ben Khalaf Tabrizi, whose penname was Borhan, *Borhan-Qate'* is a Persian dictionary first published in 1818 in Calcutta. It has been republished numerous times since its first edition and is frequently used as an authoritative reference.

Breaking-of the-Fast Cannon: Prior to the 20th century, in many large cities, a cannon was fired to announce the time for certain rituals or events, such as breaking the fast in the Islamic lunar month of Ramazan at the moment after sunset.

Bundahishn: A most important book written in Middle Persian, *Bundahishn* [Primal Creation] outlines Zoroastrian beliefs regarding cosmology and the myth of creation.

Chaharshanbeh Suri: On the Tuesday evening before the last Wednesday before the Persian New Year, Iranians observe the ancient annual custom of all souls, similar to All Souls Day, or Halloween, the evening before All Saints Day. On that evening, they make bonfires to jump over, symbolic of the ancient belief that the fire will cleanse them, that they will give all sicknesses to the fire and receive health instead. They also disguise themselves: traditionally, women wear men's clothes and men disguise themselves in women's clothes, and they go to the houses in the neighborhood with a pot and a spoon, beating on the pot, and collecting rice and various beans with which they make a thick soup, similar to what is known as "Stone Soup" in the West. They also serve a mixture of seven nuts and dried fruits, such as almonds, walnuts, and hazelnuts, and dried fruits such as apricots, peaches, and figs, called *Ajil-e Chaharshanbeh Suri*.

Chelleh: A derivative of *chehel* [forty], a *chelleh* refers to a period of 40 days and nights. An example is *chelleh-neshini*, which means going into seclusion for a period of 40 days and nights. But the word is also used for other purposes. Traditionally, winter in Persian culture is divided to two parts, called *chelleh-ye bozorg* [big *chelleh*] and *chelleh-ye kuchek* [small *chelleh*]. Big *chelleh* begins on December 21 and ends on January 29, which is forty full days, and small *chelleh* begins on January 30 and ends on February 18. which is 20 full days.

Chinvat Bridge: In contrast to the Islamic Serat Bridge, the Chivat Bridge is between the world of the living and the world of the dead. The belief is that right after death, the person's soul must cross the Chinvat Bridge. For evil doers, the bridge appears extremely narrow and impassable, while for those of good thoughts, good words, and good deeds, the bridge is quite wide and they can pass over it with ease.

Darab Pahlan: A Zoroastrian priest, Darab Pahlan (1668-1734) was the author of *Farziyyatnameh*, which outlines the duties of a Zoroastrian from birth to death.

Denkard: Written in the 10th century AD, *Denkard* [Acts of Religion] is described as an encyclopedia of Zoroastrian beliefs and customs. For more, see: *Dēnkard* in *Encyclopedia Iranica* online.

Eshpokhtor: Persian name, a corruption of "inspector," used for the Russian military commander Pavel Dmitrievich Tsitsianov during the early years of the Russo-Persian War of 1804-1813. He was assassinated in 1806, and reportedly his head was sent to Fathali Shah.

Falakossa'adeh: A 19th century Persian book of astrology and astronomy by Aliqoli Mirza E'tezadossaltaneh, the 54th son of Fathali Shah.

Farasnameh: A genre of books in Persian that deal with horses, training horses, types of horses, and any other kind of knowledge related to horses.

Fatemeh: For Shi'ites, the daughter of the Prophet Mohammad, Fatemeh Zahra, is the most revered of all women. Her husband, Ali, and her two sons, Hasan and Hoseyn, were the first three imams, and all the other nine imams as well as all seyyeds are from her lineage. She is often referred to by her epithet, Zahra [radiant].

Fathali Shah: The second Qajar monarch, who ruled Persia from 1797 to 1834.

Feast of Ghadir: Usually referred to as Ghadir-e Khomm, is the anniversary of the day in 632 CE when, according to Shi'ites, the Prophet Mohammad appointed his cousin and son-in-law, Ali, as his successor.

Feast of Sacrifices Day: or *Eyd-e Qorban*, is the 10th day of the Islamic lunar month of Zihajjeh, when the Hajj pilgrimage is performed.

Festival of Mehregan: Celebrated in the Persian month of Mehr (early October) for several days, this festival honors the Zoroastrian deity, Mithra, and is a celebration of autumn.

Festival of Nowruz: Literally, "New Day," Nowruz marks the first day of the Persian calendar year and is celebrated from the first day of Spring for thirteen days.

Festival of Sadeh: This Zoroastrian festival is celebrated 50 nights and 50 days before Nowruz. It is a celebration that starts in late January in honor of fire, to drive away the forces of evil, cold, and darkness.

Forty-Key Bowl: A metal bowl with prayers engraved around it and 40 small key-shaped pieces of metal hanging from its edge.

Gheladush: A castle, the ruins of which are near Larijan.

Ghiyas ol-Loghat: Early 19th century Persian dictionary by Ghiyas al-Din Mohammad ibn Jalal al-Din Rampuri.

Haft Sin [Seven S]: For Nowruz, or Persian New Year, in Iran, every household sets a *Haft Sin*, a table of various items including seven ingredients the names of which start with the letter S in Persian. These symbolic items typically include *sabzeh* (lentil or wheat sprouts), representing the rebirth of nature; *samanu*, a thick sweet paste made of slowly-cooked wheat sprouts; *sib* (apples); *senjed*, the fruit of the oleaster tree; *sir* (garlic), representing medicine; *somaq* (sumac); *serkeh* (vinegar), representing age and patience. *Sekkeh* (coins) can also be substituted for one of the items on the *Haft Sin*. Other items traditionally placed on a *Haft Sin* table include: painted eggs, a goldfish in a bowl of water, a brazier for burning wild rue, a pot of flowering *sonbol* (hyacinth), which can also be substituted for one of the items starting with the letter S, in addition to a mirror and two candlesticks.

Hajji: Also Hajj, an honorific used for males who have made a pilgrimage to Mecca as well as those born on the Day of Sacrifices, when the pilgrimage takes place.

Hajji Baba: *The Adventures of Hajji Baba of Ispahan* by the British author, James Morier, is a satirical novel published in 1824. For more detail, see *Encyclopædia Iranica* online.

Hamzeh-Esfahani: Abu Abdollah Hameh ibn Hasan was a Persian historian and philologist during the Abbasid era (1261-1517 AD). His most important book is a history of Isfahan.

Harun Velayat: This Safavid era mausoleum, located in the ancient square in Isfahan, is thought to be the tomb of the son of either the seventh or the tenth Shi'ite imam. It is also known as a place capable of miracles and is revered by not only Muslims but also Jews and Armenian Christians.

Ibn Moljam: The man who assassinated Imam Ali with a sword dipped in poison in 661 CE.

Ibn Muqaffa': An 8th century Persian literary scholar who translated several books from Middle Persian into Arabic. His Arabic prose translation of *Kalileh and Demneh* is regarded as a ground-breaking eloquent literary work in that language.

Ibn Sa'd: Omar ibn Sa'd was a military commander who, along with 4,000 fighters, killed Imam Hoseyn and all the members of his small army in Karbala in 580 CE on the order of the governor of Kufa, Obeydollah ibn Ziyad, and then had his horsemen ride over the corpses of Hoseyn and his followers.

Imam Zakariya ibn Mohammad ibn Mahmud Qazvini: A 13th century cosmographer and geographer, Qazvini's most famous work is *Ajayeb al-Makhlughat* [Wonders of Creation]. He is also the author of *Asar al-Belad*.

Imamzadeh: Literally, an immediate offspring of one of the twelve Shi'ite imams or their shrines. There are hundreds of such shrines in Iran, but only very few of the shrines can be authenticated as tombs of the true children of one of the imams.

Jahangiri Dictionary: or *Farhang-e Jahangiri*, was compiled by Jamal al-Din Injavi-Shirazi for the Indian King Akbar Shah in the 17th century, and when completed, it was presented to his son, Jahangir.

Jannat al-Kholud: A Persian book by Mohammad Reza ibn Mo'men-Khatunabadi, including the names of God, a brief history of prophets and imams and kings, as well as issues regarding travel, finding the Qibla, and so on, first published in 1850.

Ka'b al-Ahbar: A Yemeni Jew who converted to Islam and was closely associated with the second and third caliphs, Omar and Osman. His name is often mispronounced in Iran as "Ka'b al-Akhbar." When someone is referred to by this name, it is an expression used for a person who seems to or pretends to know everything that has happened or will happen.

Kachi: This is a very popular pudding that is served on many religious occasions. *Kachi* is prepared by browning wheat flour in butter, then adding sugar and saffron and simmering it.

Kachi-ye Ghighnagh: A very oily pudding made from flour, butter, and saffron, to which eggs cooked with brown sugar are added.

Kayanians: or members of the Kiani Dynasty in Iranian legends and mythology, especially highlighted in Ferdowsi's *Shahnameh*.

Kermani, Mirza Aqa Khan: An Iranian intellectual reformer. The writing of Mirza Aqa Khan Kermani (1854-1897) helped set the stage for the 1906-1911 Persian Constitutional Revolution.

Khaqani: A major Persian poet of the 12th century, Khaqani's fame is mostly due to his masterful odes, but also his travel memoir, *Tohfat al-Eraqayn*.

Kharbozeh **Melon**: Several varieties of an elongated Persian melon which differ in color and taste from different regions of Iran. A Mashhad or Khorasan *kharbozeh* usually has a green rind and green flesh, whereas another version cultivated in central Iran, especially around Isfahan, has a golden rind and cream-colored flesh. The taste is similar to but more flavorful than honeydew melon.

Khezr: He is a mythical figure dressed in green, a prophet/saint character in Iranian and Islamic mystic tradition who is associated with Elijah; he is believed to have drunk the Water of Life from the Fountain of Youth, and is believed to remain alive until the end of time. For a brief historical account of Khezr, see: Oliver Leaman, *The Qur'an: An Encyclopedia*.

Kianian: The Kiani Dynasty is in the mythological part of the *Book of Kings*.

King of Kheybar: Reference is to Imam Ali, who conquered the Jewish settlement in Arabia in 628 CE.

Kolayni: Mohammad ibn Ya'qub ibn Eshaq Kolayni-Razi was a 9th-10th century hadith scholar and the author of *Ketab al-Kafi*. He was a contemporary of the twelfth Shi'ite imam, Mahdi, who is believed by Shi'ites to be in occultation.

Komaj **Bread**: A type of sweetened flatbread, or pie, which is usually made with wheat flour and sugar, but it is also made with rice flour. In previous centuries, this bread was more elaborate, but the modern version of *komaj*, which is around 10" in diameter, is merely topped with sesame seeds and sweetened with a light simple syrup seasoned with saffron.

Korsi: This is a traditional apparatus for keeping warm inside a house during cold weather, consisting of a low, square table underneath which a clay brazier of crushed charcoal is placed; a large square quilt or blanket is spread over the table and overhangs on all sides, with small mattresses and cushions arranged on all four sides. Family members sit around the table with the quilt or blanket covering their laps during meals and other gatherings. The small mattresses and cushions are also used for sleeping at the sides of the *korsi*.

Kreuger: Ivar Kreuger was a Swedish financier con artist in the 1920s. See: *The Match King: Ivar Kreuger, The Financial Genius Behind a Century of Wall Street Scandals* by Frank Partnoy (2010).

Majma' al-Nureyn: Book written in Arabic by Abolhasan Marandi.

Malek Ashtar: One of the companions of the Prophet Mohammad, who gained prominence during the caliphate of Ali.

Mas'ud Sa'd Salman: An 11th century Persian poet, Mas'ud Sa'd Salman is mostly famous for his prison poems, which was the outcome of having spent almost two decades of his life in prison and exile.

Meadows of Gold and Mines of Gems: This is an English translation of *al-Zahab wa Ma'aden al-Jowhar* by the 10th century Arab historian, Al-Masudi.

Me'raj: or Ascension, refers to the Islamic belief that the Prophet Mohammad took a night journey to the heavens.

Mokarram-Esfahani: Mohammad Ali Mokarram-Esfahani [known locally as Mokrem] was a satirist who often targeted superstitious beliefs (such as miracles performed by the person buried in Harun Velayat mausoleum) in an Isfahani accent.

Mokhtar: Reference is to Mokhtar ibn Abi Obaydeh, who in 686 AD rose against the Umayyad Dynasty to avenge the killing of Imam Hoseyn and his supporters in Karbala.

Monarjonban: See: Shaking Minarets.

Murchehkhor: Colloquially Murchehkhor, but correctly Murchehkhort, is a historic village 15 kilometers north of Isfahan, with one of the largest fortresses in Iran. Part of its reputation is due to having served as the site of the battle between Nader (who later became Nader Shah Afshar) and the Afghan invaders in 1729 AD.

Naqqarehkhaneh: This is a place in some cities such as Tehran and some holy shrines such as that of Imam Reza in Mashhad in which they play the *naqqareh*, which consists of a large and a small drum, sometimes accompanied by horn instruments, usually at sunup and sundown.

Narshakhi: Abu Bakr Narshakhi, a Sogdian scholar and the author of *Tarikh-e Bokhara* [History of Bukhara], regarded as the first historian in Central Asia.

Nesab: or *Nesab al-Sabiyan*, an Arabic-Persian lexicon in verse written by Abu Nasr Farahi in the 14th century, which was used even as late as the 20th century in elementary education.

Nowruznameh: Attributed to Omar Khayyam in Persian, this book is about the origin, traditions, and customs of Persian New Year and how Iranian kings and various social classes celebrated it.

Nozhat ol-Qolub: A 14th century book by Hamdollah Mostowfi, described as an encyclopedic work dealing with topics such as astrology, geography, geology, botany, biology, and zoology, among others.

Pir-e Palanduz: Meaning, Old Saddlemaker, reference to Sheykh Mohammad Karandehi, a Safavid era dervish, whose mausoleum in Mashhad is a Shi'ite tourist and pilgrimage attraction.

Prophet Hud: It is stated in the surah "Al-A'raf" [The Heights], verse 65, of the Koran: "And unto the tribe of Ad, We sent their brother Hud."

Prophet Saleh: It is stated in the surah "Hur," verse 61, of the Koran: "And unto the tribe of Thamud, We sent their brother Saleh."

Omm al-Bani: Possibly a reference to Omm al-Banin, the mother of Imam Reza, who is the only Shi'ite imam buried in Iran.

Qabusnameh: A book in the "mirrors of princes" genre written in the 11th century by Kaykavus ibn Eskandar, the ruler of Tabarestan, for his son

Qanat: Also called *kariz*, is an ancient Persian water source and irrigation system consisting of gently sloping underground tunnels or channels dug in order to direct water from the inside of a hill to a village below for drinking and farming.

Qavanin al-Sayyad: Possibly a reference to *Seyd al-Morad fi Qavanin al-Sayyad*, an 18 century study of animals and guide for training birds by Khodayar Khan Sendi, first published by Baptist Mission Press in Calcutta, India in 1908.

Qavut: a mixture of roasted chickpea flour and sugar, *qavut* is served in small saucers with small spoons for each individual and is usually one of the features of certain religious ceremonies. Varieties of *qavut* are made with the same mixture, with added aromatic spices such as cardamom and cinnamon.

Qesas al-Olama: Written by Mohammad ibn Soleyman Tonokaboni, this book consists of biographies of 153 Shi'ite religious scholars, mostly from the Safavid Dynasty era.

Religiously Clean [*Pak*]: A woman who is not undergoing menstruation, lochia, or menorrhagia, and who has performed full ablution after sexual intercourse, or a man who has performed full ablution after sexual intercourse or ejaculation.

Religiously Unclean [*Napak*]: A woman who is undergoing menstruation, lochia, or menorrhagia, and who has not performed full ablution after sexual intercourse, or a man who has not performed full ablution after sexual intercourse or ejaculation.

Rostam: In the mythological part of the *Book of Kings*, Rostam is the greatest of Persian heroes.

Sad Dar: "As its name implies the *Sad Dar* is a treatise on 'a hundred subjects' connected with the Zoroastrian religion. The word *dar*, literally 'door, or gate,' being also applied to the chapters of a book, and to the 'matters, or subjects,' of which it treats. This work is not a Pahlavi text, being written in Persian with an admixture of about four per cent of Arabic words; it is, however, more quoted than any other work by the Parsi compilers of the Persian Rivayats, or religious 'traditions,' in the seventeenth century." (From the Introduction by E. W. West)

Sad Dar Bundehesh: Published in India in 1909, along with *Sad Dar Nasr*, *Sad Dar Bundehesh* is a book about Zoroastrian teachings, rituals, and obligations.

Sad Dar Nasr: Also published in India in 1909, *Sad Dar Nasr* is about Zoroastrian teachings and folk and religious beliefs.

Safavid Dynasty: This dynasty ruled Iran from 1576-1732 CE.

Salaman and Absal: A doomed romance in verse by 15th century Persian poet Jami. It was translated into English by the 19th century English poet Edward Fitzgerald.

Samanu: A dish that is usually prepared in early spring, and is one of the items placed on the *Haft Sin* for Persian New Year (Nowruz). It is made with whole wheat soaked in water for several days to sprout, which then is simmered slowly for many hours; then wheat flour is added to make it into a sweet brown paste.

Sassanid Empire: 224-651 CE.

Seh Maktub: Literally "three essays," is the title of an influential book by the 19th century reformist, Mirza Aqa Khan Kermani.

Serat Bridge: Akin to the Zoroastrian Chinvat Bridge, it is believed to be a bridge thinner than a hair and sharper than a sword over which every person must pass to reach Paradise on Resurrection Day. Since it is over the fires of Hell, sinners burn and fall into Hell, but the faithful can cross it to Paradise unharmed.

Seyyed: an honorific used before the names of males whose lineage is from the family of the Prophet Mohammad.

Shab-e Yalda (Winter Solstice): *Shab-e Yalda*, the winter solstice, is the longest night of the year. Marking the rebirth of the sun, this festival is traced to the Zoroastrian concept of light and good in opposition to darkness and evil. On *Shab-e Yalda*, family and friends gather for a night-long vigil around the traditional winter heating apparatus called a *korsi* (see *korsi* in this section). In older times, when fresh fruits were not available in winter, families carefully saved all sorts of fruits, especially watermelon, to serve to guests on this night. A variety of sweets and other foods are also served to celebrate *Shab-e Yalda*.

Shahi: In the early- to mid-20th century, a small unit of currency akin to an American nickel.

Shaking Minarets: This monument is the tomb of a 14th century Sufi ascetic, which was renovated during the Safavid era. When a person climbs up the inside stairs of one of the two minarets and grabs the windowsill and shakes the minaret, the other minaret also shakes.

Sham-e Ghariban: literally "the night of lonely strangers," is a commemoration of the evening of Ashra, when almost all the men of Imam Hoseyn's army were killed and the women and children of his camp became prisoners of his enemies.

Shayest Nashayest: Literally "proper, improper," is book written in the Middle Persian [Pahlavi] language, which is comprised of some of the most important religious jurisprudential dictums of the Sassanid era.

Shemr: Shemr ibn Zi al-Jowshan, one of the most reviled figures in Shi'ite lore, was the killer of Imam Hoseyn in the Battle of Karbala in 680 CE.

Sheshandaz: Although according to Dehkhoda's *Encyclopedic Dictionary*, this dish was an egg-drop soup with onions, in recent decades, varieties of *sheshandaz* appear in cookbooks that are similar to vegetable soufflés, with eggs cooked on top.

Sheykh Baha'i: A 16th-17th century Shi'ite scholar, poet, philosopher, mathematician, astronomer, and architect, who is credited with the design of some of the major monuments and urban designs in Isfahan during the Safavid era.

Shrine of Shah Abdolazim: The most important Imamzadeh in the city of Rey in greater Tehran today, it is the tomb of a 9th century descendent of the second Shi'ite Imam, Hasan, and the site of the mausoleums of many notable figures in Iran's history.

Simorgh: A benevolent mythological bird, Simorgh is frequently found in Persian legends, art, and literature, such as *Mateqolteyer* by the 12th-13th century Persian poet, Attar. For an English translation of this work, see Farid Ud-din Attar, *The Conference of the Birds*, translated by Afkham Darbandi and Dick Davis (London: Penguin, 1984).

Sir: A more or less outmoded measure of weight, equivalent to about 80 grams. See: *Astir*.

Sofreh (**Banquet**): The term *sofreh*, which literally means "supper cloth," implies a dinner or luncheon party. Such a party is given on various occasions, such as celebrating a circumcision or a wedding, or for religious purposes. A religious *sofreh* is usually organized and attended by women. In every *sofreh,* candles are used for decoration, and bread, water, and dates are served. Bread represents a blessing from God, while dates are important as they were one of the favorite foods of the Prophet Mohammad, and water is the source of life. Water is also an important symbolic element in the Shi'i tradition, since it is associated with the Battle of Karbala in which the third imam of the Shi'ites, Hoseyn, and many members of his family were prevented from having access to water and were ultimately killed. Candles represent God, the Illuminator.

Sudgar Nask: The first part of the Sassanid Avesta.

Tarikh-e Bokhara [History of Bukhara]: Written in Arabic in the 10th century by the Sogdian scholar, Abu Bakr Narshakhi, and presented to the Samanid king, Nuh I.

Turanians: People of Turan, which, according to the *Shahnameh*, were the adversaries of Iranians.

Vendidad: A collection of texts within the Avesta, which describes rules involving such things as demons as well as pollution and mostly deals with jurisprudence (including health and ritual issues). The Vendidad is one of the most rooted and fundamental elements of Iranian religious myths.

Water of Life: Persian literature, especially mystic literature, contains stories about Alexander of Macedonia, who, accompanied by the Prophet Khezr, went to the Region of Darkness in search of the Water of Life (Fountain of Youth). Among other sources, this legend is told in Ferdowsi's *Book of Kings* and Nezami's 12th century *Eskandarnameh*. For an English translation of Nezami's work, see: Minoo S. Southgate, trans., *Iskandarnamah: A Persian Medieval Alexander-Romance* (New York: Columbia University Press, 1978).

Yana Bei' al-Islam: A translation of *The Original Sources of The Qur'an: Its Origin in Pagan Legends and Mythology* by William St. Clair Tisdall in 1905. Tisdall, who was fluent in several Middle Eastern languages and served as a missionary in Isfahan, was a British Anglican priest. Several books were written in Iran to refute his claims.

Yasin Ring: A large piece of cloth used in rituals, on the four corners of which the names of the Prophet Mohammad, his daughter Fatemeh, her husband Ali, and their sons Hasan and Hoseyn are written. In the middle of the cloth, a hole is cut large enough to put one's head through.

Zahhak: Also Azhidehak, is perhaps the most evil character in the *Book of Kings*. Zahhak was kissed on his shoulders by Ahriman (Satan), which caused black serpents to grow out from his shoulders, for the feeding of which they required two human brains each day.

Zaratosht Bahram: or Zartosht Bahram, an important 13th century Persian Zoroastrian poet and the author of *Zartosht-nameh* and *Ardavirafnameh.*

Zoljanah: Name of Imam Hoseyn's horse, which was apparently bred and raised by the Prophet Mohammad. It was killed during the Battle of Karbala.

Index

About the Translator

M. R. Ghanoonparvar is Professor Emeritus of Persian and Comparative Literature at The University of Texas at Austin. Professor Ghanoonparvar has also taught at the University of Isfahan, the University of Virginia, and the University of Arizona, and was a Rockefeller Fellow at the University of Michigan. He is the recipient of a Lifetime Achievement Award from the American Association of Teachers of Persian (2021) as well as a Lifetime Achievement Award for his contributions to presenting Persian culinary arts to the non-Iranian public from *Encyclopædia Iranica* (2009). He has published widely on Persian literature and culture in both English and Persian and is the author of: *Prophets of Doom: Literature as a Socio-Political Phenomenon in Modern Iran* (1984), *In a Persian Mirror: Images of the West and Westerners in Iranian Fiction* (1993), *Translating the Garden* (2001), *Reading Chubak* (2005), *Persian Cuisine: Traditional, Regional and Modern Foods* (2006), *Iranian Film and Persian Fiction* (2016), *Dining at the Safavid Court* (2016), *From Prophets of Doom to Chroniclers of Gloom* (2021), and *Iranian Cities in Persian Fiction* (2022). His translations include Jalal Al-e Ahmad's *By the Pen*, Sadeq Chubak's *The Patient Stone*, Simin Daneshvar's *Savushun*, Ahmad Kasravi's *On Islam and Shi'ism*, Sadeq Hedayat's *The Myth of Creation*, Nima Yushij's *The Neighbor Says: Letters of Nima Yushij and the Philosophy of Modern Persian Poetry*, Davud Ghaffarzadegan's *Fortune Told in Blood*, Mohammad Reza Bayrami's *The Tales of Sabalan* and *Eagles of Hill 60*, and Bahram Beyza'i's *Memoirs of the Actor in a Supporting Role*. His edited volumes include *Iranian Drama: An Anthology*, *In Transition: Essays on Culture and Identity in Middle Eastern Societies*, Gholamhoseyn Sa'edi's *Othello in Wonderland and Mirror-Polishing Storytellers*, and Moniro Ravanipour's *Satan Stones* and *Kanizu*. His most recent translations include Shahrokh Meskub's *In the Alley of the Friend* and *Leaving, Staying, Returning*, Hushang Golshiri's *Book of Jinn*, Moniro Ravanipour's *The Drowned* and *These Crazy Nights*, Hamid Shokat's *Flight into Darkness: A Political Biography of Shapour*

Bakhtiar and *Caught in the Crossfire: A Political Biography of Qavamossaltaneh*, Ghazaleh Alizadeh's *The Nights of Tehran* and *Two Views and Trial* Ruhangiz Sharifian's *The Last Dream* and *Doran*, and Shahrnush Parsipur's *Blue Logos*. He was the recipient of the 2008 Lois Roth Prize for Literary Translation. His forthcoming books are *Diseases, Dying, and Death in Persian Stories* and *A River of Memories: A Memoir of Life and Literature.* His forthcoming translations include Ghazaleh Alizadeh's *The House of the Edrisis*, Hossein Atashparvar's *From the Moon to the Well*, and Reza Julai's *Jujube Blossoms*.

List of books by Sadeq Hedayat published by this press

Tup-e Morvari
[The Pearl Cannon]
Edited by Iraj Bashiri
(1985)

The Myth of Creation
Translated by M. R. Ghanoonparvar
Illustrated by Kaya Behkalam
(1998)

Of Rated Interest

The Fiction of Sadeq Hedayat
Iraj Bashiri
(1984)

Hedayat on Religion
M. R. Ghanoonparvar and Paul Sprachman
(2024)

About Mazda Publishers

Since its establishment in 1980, Mazda Publishers has built a strong reputation for excellence in both scholarly and trade publishing. The company has consistently produced high-quality texts, reference materials, literary works, and general interest books aimed at both researchers and the general public. Mazda's diverse catalog spans a wide array of subjects, including art and architecture, politics, religion, history, language, and culture.

At the heart of Mazda Publishers' mission lies the study of what we refer to as the Iranicas—an academic exploration of the many facets of Iranian civilization throughout history. This includes not only the political, social, and cultural dimensions of the Iranian world, but also the broader influence of Iranian elements across regions and time periods. While modern Iran is central to this focus, Mazda Publishers also explores the enduring legacy of Iranian civilization in areas beyond its contemporary borders—reaching from ancient China to the Mediterranean shores. This broad approach is essential due to the inclusive and eclectic nature of Iranian civilization.

In line with this vision, Mazda Publishers has produced works on a variety of subjects, including the history and cultures of Armenia, Tajikistan, Afghanistan, and the countries surrounding the Persian Gulf. The publishing house has also explored themes in Islamic studies, Zoroastrianism, Jewish history, the Kurdish people, Ottoman Turkey, Mughal India, and Egypt, among others. This ongoing commitment to expanding the scope of Iranian studies ensures that Mazda will continue to produce vital and diverse scholarship for years to come.

About the Publisher

Dr. A. K. Jabbari, the founder of Mazda Publishers, is a distinguished figure in the field of Iranian studies. Holding a B.S. and M.S. in Aerospace Engineering from Pennsylvania State University, as well as a Ph.D. in Economics from Washington University in St. Louis, Dr. Jabbari has significantly contributed to the dissemination of scholarly works on Iran and Persian culture.

Through Mazda Publishers, Dr. Jabbari has played a pivotal role in expanding the availability of academic resources on a range of topics related to Iran and its historical and cultural spheres. The publishing house has produced numerous books on Persian literature, history, art, philosophy, and linguistics, becoming an invaluable resource for scholars, researchers, and enthusiasts alike. Under Dr. Jabbari's leadership, Mazda Publishers has earned a reputation as a respected and trusted source in the field of Iranian studies.

For more informaion please visit www.mazdapublishers.com